GREATEST
BEERS
OF THE WORLD

IN ASSOCIATION WITH
TIMPSON

GREATEST
BEERS
OF THE WORLD

TIM HAMPSON

Published in the UK in 2016 by
Icon Books Ltd, Omnibus Business Centre,
39–41 North Road, London N7 9DP
email: info@iconbooks.com
www.iconbooks.com

Sold in the UK, Europe and Asia
by Faber & Faber Ltd, Bloomsbury House,
74–77 Great Russell Street,
London WC1B 3DA or their agents

Distributed in the UK, Europe and Asia
by Grantham Book Services, Trent Road,
Grantham NG31 7XQ

Distributed in Australia and New Zealand
by Allen & Unwin Pty Ltd,
PO Box 8500, 83 Alexander Street,
Crows Nest, NSW 2065

Distributed in South Africa by
Jonathan Ball, Office B4, The District,
41 Sir Lowry Road, Woodstock 7925

Distributed in India by Penguin Books India,
7th Floor, Infinity Tower – C, DLF Cyber City,
Gurgaon 122002, Haryana

Distributed in Canada by Publishers Group Canada,
76 Stafford Street, Unit 300, Toronto, Ontario M6J 2S1

Distributed in the USA by Publishers Group West,
1700 Fourth Street, Berkeley, CA 94710

ISBN: 978-178578-109-4

Images – see individual pictures

Typeset and designed by Simmons Pugh

Printed and bound in the UK by Clays Ltd, St Ives plc

ABOUT THE AUTHOR

Tim Hampson has travelled the world in search of the perfect beer, a quest he hopes will continue for many more years. His previous books include *World Beer, The Beer Book*, the *Haynes Beer Manual, London's Best Pubs, 101 Beer Days Out* and *Great Beers*. He is the Chairman of the British Guild of Beer Writers, and in 2015 he was knighted by the Belgian Brewers' Guild for services to beer culture. Tim lives in Oxford together with his family, three dogs and a parrot.

CONTENTS

INTRODUCTION

The 50 greatest beers in the world? The question is absurd. But within the embrace of the absurdity lies a gem of an idea.

We've been drinking beers for more than 10,000 years. And for most of that time people just drank beer that was probably made at home or in a communal brewery. The evolution of beer styles and beer names is a relatively recent activity.

In recent times, for those of us who drink beer, it has often unerringly helped shape who we are. Many remember the first beer they drank as an underage youth. Others have fond recollections of sitting with a parent in a pub and drinking their first legal (or illegal) beer. For many, their university years are marked and remembered by the beers they drank. And years later, like some Proustian remembrance of days past, the memories will come back of the beers, the company and conversations. There are the great moments of time marked by the tastes and aromas of the beers people drank.

But 50 great beers? Some might argue such a list should be solely compiled from Britain's rich tapestry of beers. But this narrow, jingoistic view of the beer world would exclude all the other countries where great beers are made and drunk. Beer culture is not limited to the United Kingdom and there are a number of internationally recognised beer brands and many countries have their own thriving brewing industry.

So will people from other countries find their favourite beers here? An Australian might expect to see VB, an Italian might look for Peroni Nastro Azzurro, some Belgians Jupiler or Stella Artois. Americans may ask where is the Budweiser or even the Miller Lite? A Brazilian might expect to find their beloved Brahma, perhaps someone from China will look for Snow. These beers are all well loved and well known, and they are sold by the bucketful. But volume doesn't make greatness and familiarity doesn't guarantee inclusion in this book.

Choosing the beers for this book has been no easy task. Britain alone has more than 1,500 breweries, the USA has 3,500, wine-loving Italy more than 700. On just about every continent from the Arctic down to the Antarctic, there are people brewing great beer. The number of beers being brewed is big and daily increasing.

So how to make it into my eclectic list of 50 great beers?

I've travelled the world drinking beers and sat with many brewers discussing and analysing their creations, marvelling at how from such simple notes – malt, hops, water and yeast – a symphony of tastes and colours can be created. If there is a link between any of the beers in this book, it is that they in some way have made a contribution to evolving beer culture or are an exemplar of a particular beer style, or they are one of those beers that should be sought out by any beer fan just because they are so good to drink.

I imagine the first thing many people will do when they pick up this book will be to look at the contents list. They may be elated on finding a favourite beer. Many will be disappointed. But not being listed in this book doesn't make their favourite beer bad.

But a beer's inclusion or exclusion could spark a conversation as to which are the greatest beers in the world. Beer brings people together; it is a liquid social lubricant that encourages us to talk and put the world to rights. And that is perhaps one definition of what makes a great beer everyone could agree about: the company of friends and conversation – it's what life is all about.

THE BREWING PROCESS

B rewing is a simple, natural process, normally just using water, cereal, hops and yeast. Fermentable sugars are extracted from a cereal using warm water, a process known as mashing. The liquid is then brought to boiling point and hops are added for flavour, bitterness and to ward off bacteria. It is then cooled, more hops might be added, yeast is added and the fermentation process begins – converting the sugar into carbon dioxide and the alcohol we call beer.

1. MALTING
Before the grain gets to the brewery, it has to be malted. The process unlocks the complex sugars found in molecules of starch. To begin the process of releasing the sugars the maltster soaks the grains (steeps) and then gently heats them to begin the process of germination, creating simpler sugars. Inside the grain, as the seed starts to grow, the starch is broken down into simpler compounds. After a few days, the germination is stopped and the malt is dried and kilned. The more intense the kilning, the darker is the malt. The once hard grains are now soft enough to chew on and their sweetness can be tasted.

2. MILLING
In the brewery or at the maltsters, whole malted barley and other grains are ground in a mill. The cracked grain is

known as grist and it is easier for it to release its sugars at the next stage when it is wetted, in warm water. The choice of grains made by the brewer is known as the grain bill and it is important because it will affect the amount of alcohol in the beer, its colour and its taste. Lighter coloured malts help make lagers pale. Dark roasted grains give stouts their blackness.

3. MASHING
The grist is mixed with hot water in a vessel known as a tun to produce a sweet-smelling mash. The porridge-like mash is then left to stand – the process is similar to mashing a tea with warm water in a teapot. The heat of the water draws the sugars out of the malt. This is known as a single infusion mashing. Some brewers take off some of the liquid and run it off into another vessel, heat it to a higher temperature and put it back into the tun, once, twice or even three times. This is known as decoction mashing. The higher temperatures draw out even sweeter, more complex sugars from the malt.

4. BOILING
At the end of the mashing, the sugar-rich, sweet wort is strained through the bottom of the spent grains, or everything passes into a large sieve called a lauter tun. As the sweet wort runs off, the grain is rinsed (sparged) with more hot water to release the final sugars from the malt. The wort now passes into a brew kettle, or copper. The temperature is brought up to boiling point and the liquid is boiled for about an hour. Hops are added at different times for aroma and bitterness, and to stop unwanted bacterial activity. Boiling also sterilises the liquid. Some brewers add other herbs and spices at this stage.

5. FERMENTATION

The hopped wort is next strained to remove the hop residue. Then it's rapidly cooled by passing through a heat exchanger. The wort is now put into a fermenting vessel. If it is too warm the yeast will die; too cold and the yeast will take a long time to do its work. The yeast is put into the wort (pitched) and now the real magic of brewing begins: as part of its lifecycle yeast produces carbon dioxide and alcohol from the sugar and millions more yeast cells.

6. CONDITIONING

Once fermentation is finished, a process that can take four or five days, the liquid is known as green beer. It is removed, leaving most of the yeast behind, and put (racked) into another vessel. It is given time to condition and mature; during this time a secondary fermentation will take place. All the time the flavours of the beer are maturing and evolving. The beer is then put into a cask, keg, bottle or can, though keller beers will be served straight from the conditioning tank straight into a bar. Some beers are clarified, others are served unfiltered. Some are pasteurised and others are not. But one thing is certain – they're all beers.

BEER STYLES

B eer is just beer, isn't it? Well, not quite. From light American lagers to easy-drinking English pale ales, through to big, bold beers aged in whisky wood, the world of beer is wide and varied. There are dark ales, golden-hued lagers, fruity beers, hoppy beers, cloudy beers, herb beers, spicy beers and there are wild yeast-inspired creations. And they are all beers. Beer is anything but bland. According to the American Brewers Association, there are more than 80 different beer styles, many with extensive subdivisions, and the number is continuing to grow.

The beer family falls into three broad genres, which are usually defined by the yeast used: ale, lager or wild.

ALES

Traditionally, ales are beers that have a warmer fermentation than a lager. Most ales are produced using a yeast strain called *Saccharomyces cerevisiae*. As part of its lifecycle the yeast cell feeds off the sugar in the sweet wort, producing ethanol alcohol and carbon dioxide. Many years ago, members of the ale family were typically fermented at 15–25°C, but today, with a better understanding of brewing technology, the temperature beer is brewed at is no longer style-defining. Ale yeasts are often described as top fermenting, but top cropping would probably be a better description: the yeast ferments at all levels throughout the liquid, but once its work is done it collects at the top of the fermenting vessel (traditionally these vessels would have been open at the top). Family members include bitters, porters, stouts, alts and kölschs. Typically, one should expect fruity flavours.

LAGER

Lager is the world's most popular beer style, though it could be argued it's a production process rather than a style. Lager beers are a far wider range of beers than some might expect. The category doesn't just include yellow beers served at ice-cold temperatures. The word lager means to store at a cold temperature, though there is no accepted definition of what temperature or how long for. Lager beers are traditionally fermented at cooler temperatures than other beers, often 5–9°C, and then matured or stored at close to freezing, 0°C, but today many brewers are using warmer fermentation temperatures for lagers.

Lagers are made using the yeast *Saccharomyces pastorianus*, which is often called *Saccharomyces carlsbergensis*. Lagers are often described as bottom-fermenting beers, but bottom cropping would be a better description. Once settled, the brewer can easily drain the beer away from the fermentation vessel, leaving a bed of yeast, and if needed some of this can be 'cropped' for use in the next fermentation.

Beers within the lager family include pilsners, Dort-munders, Märzen and bocks. Lagers tend to have dry, crisp, biscuit flavours.

WILD YEASTS

Within the family of beers there is a third broad style, beers that are fermented after exposure to the air, which allows wild yeasts and bacteria to infect them. Some call this a natural fermentation, when no selection of yeast has taken place. The resulting flavour is dependent on the actual microorganisms, but it is normally quite tart and tongue tingling. The lambic beers of Belgium are probably the best-known examples of spontaneous fermentation. Some breweries actually use a commercially available wild yeast, like *Brettanomyces bruxellensis*, to create more complex beers often with dry, vinous and some cidery flavours and a tart sourness.

SOME MEMBERS OF THE BEER FAMILY

ALES

Alt

Alt is a German word meaning 'old' or 'traditional'. It is a style of beer traditionally made in Düsseldorf and a few other cities in northern Germany; some bars can still be found where it is served straight from a cask. It is a dark copper beer, brewed using top fermentation.

Amber/Vienna

Viennas have a rich malt aroma and a palate balanced by light fruit and aromatic hops. A bittersweet finish with malt to the fore, but with good lingering hop notes.

Barley wine

An old English style of beer. Barley wines tend to be strong and warming – often between 10 per cent alcohol by volume ABV and 12 per cent, though less strong versions are available. Expect boiled sweet and intense dark fruit flavours.

Belgian brown

A traditional beer from the Flanders region of Belgium. The light-to-medium-bodied deep copper-brown ale typically has a slight to strong lactic sourness and is often known as an oud bruin. Framboises variants have raspberries and kriek variants have cherries added for a second fermentation.

Belgian-style dubbel
Expect rich sweet maltiness on the nose that might bring forth chocolate, toasted brioche or caramel notes; the nose also often features dried fruit such as raisins as well as a hint of pepperiness from the hop.

Belgian-style strong (including quadrupels)
Expect dark chocolate, coffee, raisins, peppery hop and warming alcohol notes on the nose; palate also features chocolate, coffee, dark fruits, expressions of malt complexity and a long characterful finish.

Bière de garde and saison
Traditional farmhouse beers from the Flanders region of France and Belgium. They can be bottle conditioned and are often sold in bottles sealed with champagne-style wired corks. The style of beer is characterised by a lightly toasted malt aroma, and some malt sweetness. The hop flavour contribution is likely to be minimal, but not necessarily so. Some sour *Brettanomyces* characters can be present. Clove flavours may be detected.

Bitter
Bitter and pale ale can be synonymous. It is a style that has been mass produced in England for more than 100 years. Bitters are generally deep bronze or copper in colour due to the use of slightly darker malts, such as crystal malts. Part of their appeal was that they could be served quickly on draught, after a few days of conditioning in the pub.

Brown ale

English brown ales are not common these days. The colour can range from copper to brown. They have a medium body and range from dry to sweet maltiness with very little hop flavour or aroma. The origin of the beer could go back to the era before hops were used by English brewers. They are likely to be darker than a bitter or pale ale, though of course Newcastle Brown Ale is the exception to this rule.

Brown ale (America)

Malt aroma features chocolate and caramel malts, rather than fermentation character. Hop aroma and bitterness medium to strong, with some versions accenting citrusy North-west American hops; 4.5–6% per cent ABV.

Cask-conditioned ale

Cask-conditioned ale or real ales are unpasteurised living beers that undergo their secondary fermentation in the container from which the beer is served. A common style in the UK, cask ales are predominately sold on draught in pubs.

Golden ale

A new style of beer developed in Britain in the 1980s to tempt drinkers away from light-coloured lagers to cask beer. Lighter in colour than a pale ale, lager malts will often be used. Flavoursome hops, from America, New Zealand or Australia, are often used in abundance. Golden ales are often full of spicy, citrus flavours. Such beers are often served at temperatures lower than 10°C.

Imperial stout

A big, bold giant of a beer, its colour goes from dark copper to black. High in alcohol, they are likely to be rich and malty and can be very sweet. Strong enough to keep for years, the complexity of the beer changes from year to year. Drinking one is never predictable, but it is rarely disappointing.

India pale ale (IPA) – US style

Originally an English pale ale, the style has been reinvigorated and reinvented by the American craft beer movement. American interpretations are often identified by being highly bittered through the massive use of citrus-flavoured hops, which is balanced with rich, juicy malt. Often the signature brew for many brewers, it is now widely brewed by craft brewers worldwide.

Black IPA

Dark in colour. Manages to combine the rich tropical fruit/ripe peach skin/grapefruit notes of a new-wave IPA with a hint of dark malts, though not too much roastiness. Palate is light and shade with big hop character (grapefruit/lychee perhaps) contrasted with a tarry (but not roast) dark maltiness. Big lasting finish.

Kölsch

Light, almost straw-coloured, this golden ale once was only brewed in Cologne, Germany. It is an ale that is served at lager temperatures and is a speciality of many brewpubs in the city. Served fresh, they should be full of light malt and floral fruit flavours, apple or pear characteristics might even be detected.

Mild

Mild was once the most popular style of beer in Britain. It was developed in the 18th and 19th centuries as a less bitter (milder) style of beer than porter and stout and was the drink of choice for generations of factory and agricultural workers wanting a refreshing drink after a day's work. Often sweet to taste, mild is usually dark brown in colour, due to the use of well-roasted malts or roasted barley, and is lightly hopped.

Milk stout/sweet stout

In the late 19th century, a taste arose for sweeter stouts. The perfection around 1907 of stouts made with an addition of unfermentable lactose sugar, which was originally derived from milk, eventually resulted in one of the most popular British beer styles of the mid-20th century.

Oatmeal stout

Warm fermented with the addition of oatmeal to the grist. Moderate bitterness and a smooth profile. Generally 3.8–4.5 per cent ABV.

Old ale

Old ale is another style with roots back in beer's distant past. Old ale can mature for months or even years in wooden vessels, where it could pick up some lactic sourness from wild Brettanomyces yeasts in the wood. Often known as winter warmers, they can also be matured for long periods in a bottle. It can have flavours of roasted grain, dark soft fruits or even fresh tobacco.

Pale ale

Pale ale was known as 'the beer of the railway age'. Pale ales were developed in Burton upon Trent during the 18th and 19th centuries and were transported around the country first by canals and then by the new railway system. Brewers from London, Liverpool and Manchester built breweries in Burton to make use of the gypsum-rich water in their own versions of pale ale. One brewer even shipped water to Manchester to brew from. Widely exported, beers sent to India became known as India Pale Ale.

Pale ale (American style)
American pale ales range from deep golden to copper in colour. The style is characterised by floral and citrus American-variety hops like Cascade, though hops from other countries can be used, to produce high hop bitterness, flavour and aroma. American strong pale ales are moderate in their body and maltiness.

Porter and stout
Porter was developed in London and was the first beer to be widely sold commercially in the early 18th century. As maltsters and brewers grew to understand how to control the roasting of barley to higher temperatures, this brown-coloured beer became darker black and often full of roasted coffee flavours. Lots of hops are usually added for bitterness. The stronger versions of porter were called stout porter or stout for short.

Rauchbier – smoked beer
A speciality of Bamberg in Germany, the smokiness of the beers derives from the use of malt smoked over beechwood. Alaskan Brewing makes a version with alder-smoked malt. Complex beers, phenolic, banana and clove flavours are often to the fore. The style pairs well with fatty meats and pickled fish.

Saison
A traditional Belgian farmhouse beer, brewed in winter for consumption in the summer months. Long storage

would often give the beer some sour notes. The style all but died out, but was revived by the US craft beer movement. Today brewers often use the style as a way of showing the contribution herbs, spices and fruits can make to a beer.

Trappist beers

Trappist beers are not a style of beer, though they are all likely to be top-fermenting, bottle-conditioned ales. However, a beer can be described as Trappist if it has been brewed within the walls of a Trappist monastery, either by the monks themselves or under their supervision. The best known Trappist beers are produced by the abbeys of Chimay, Rochefort, Orval, Westvleteren, Westmalle and Achel in Belgium and Schaapskooi in the Netherlands.

Wheat beers (Belgian style)

The Belgian and Dutch versions of wheat beers, which are known as witte or biere blanches, are usually made with the addition of herbs and spices such as ground coriander seeds and orange curaçao or orange peel. The hop presence is normally low and many believe the origins of the beer go back to mediaeval times when a herb and spice mixture (gruit) was used to flavour beers not hops.

Wheat beers (German style)

Weiss (white) or Weizen (wheat) beers are made with 40% wheat mixed with barley malt. The style is very common in Germany, especially Bavaria, but it is now a favourite of many brewers worldwide. Refreshing, crisp and usually turbid, a variation on the ale yeast produces sometimes highly pronounced banana, clove and bubblegum flavours. Unfiltered versions are called hefeweiss or hefeweizen. Filtered versions are called kristal.

Wheat variant: Berliner weisse

The lightest of the German wheat beers, they are very pale in colour and typically low in alcohol, about 3 per cent ABV. The style was at its most popular in the 19th century when more than 700 breweries produced it. Now demand for it has fallen to the extent that it has all but died out in Berlin. Sour to the taste, it is often served with flavoured syrups or woodruff.

LAGERS

American-style lager

Light in body and very light to straw in colour, American lagers are very clean and crisp, heavily carbonated and usually served very cold. The flavour components should be subtle but complex, with no one ingredient dominating. Malt sweetness is light to mild. Corn, rice or other grain or sugar adjuncts are often used. Hop bitterness, flavour and aroma are negligible to very light.

Bock and its variants

Traditional German bocks are strong, malty, medium-to-full-bodied, bottom-fermented beers. The complex flavours of malt and fruit usually dominate the taste. Doppelbock are even stronger and the triple steps up the excitement. An eisbock is one that has been made by freezing the beer in a barrel and taking out the ice to leave a stronger beer. Variants on bocks are found throughout the world, particularly in Belgium.

Bohemian or Czech pilsner

The father of a beer style that has swept the world. The

flavour of spicy and herbal hops should sing in harmony with the sweetness of the Moravian pilsner malt. They can be golden or even pale amber. Some versions of this beer are lagered for three months, but many exemplars of the style are lagered for a much shorter time. The beer should be served with a full, dense white head.

Dortmunder
Brewed around the German city of Dortmund, it is similar in style to a helles. It has a moderate hop bitterness and is not assertively malty.

German-style or continental pilsner
The classic German pilsner is golden or light straw in colour and is well hopped. The presence of hop bitterness from the use of noble hops should be medium to high. It is a well-attenuated, medium-to-light-bodied beer with malt present in the aroma and flavour. Some drinkers can detect sweetcorn flavours.

Helles
A pale lager often brewed around Munich in Germany. Usually light gold in colour, the flavours are far subtler than would be expected from a pilsner style.

Märzen
A seasonal beer from Germany, characterised by a medium body and broad range of colours. Traditionally brewed in March and stored over the summer in ice caves ready for drinking in the autumn.

Vienna-style lager
Made with a red-coloured Vienna malt, the beer is reddish brown or copper coloured. The malt dominates the aroma

and instils a sweetness into the beer. The hop bitterness is clean, crisp and relatively low.

WILD BREWS

Fruit lambic

Soft fruit such as raspberry or cherry may be added to a gueuze, but pear and blackcurrant and even banana have also been used to create these beers. Often fermented in a wooden cask, in traditional versions most of the sugars are fermented out and the beer is very dry. Some versions use fruit syrup, which often overpowers the beer's acidity.

Geuze lambic

Old lambic is blended with newly fermenting young lambic to create this beer. Light bodied, milder and sweeter than a single lambic, many people find it a more approachable beer. Additional sugar is sometimes added to the beer, which helps counter the acidity. If brown sugar is added, the beer is known as a faro.

Lambic

Unblended, naturally and spontaneously fermented lambic is intensely sour and sometimes, but not always, acetic. They are very, very dry. It is a beer that is traditionally is made in Belgium's Senne Valley. Once all beers would have been fermented in this fashion. The beer is traditionally matured in oak barrels to produce its compelling flavours. Old hops are used for preserving the beer not bittering it. A lambic will often pair unbelievably well with food.

Leipzig-Gose

A beer that is traditional to the Leipzig area of Germany. Traditionally they fermented spontaneously, similar to Belgian-style lambic beers. They are drunk young and drinkers should expert acidic lemon or other citrus-like flavours on the nose and palate. There is normally little evidence of hops or malt character.

SOME OTHER BEERS

Chocolate and coffee

Any beer made with the addition of chocolate or coffee. Aroma and palate determined by the ingredients used. The ABV ranges can vary.

Czech-style pale

Cold fermented. Ranges from pale to yellow-gold in colour; toasted grain and floral, herbal, grassy hops aromas. Ripe, juicy malt and tangy hops with light citrus fruit in the mouth. Long, lingering finish, balanced between malt dryness and tart hop bitterness. Medium body. 4–5.2% ABV.

Fruit

Any cold- or warm-fermented beer made with addition of fruit such as cherry, raspberry or peach. The aromas and palate are determined by the type of fruit added. NB: Not made by spontaneous fermentation. The ABV ranges can vary.

Fruit beer
Fruit beer is any beer made using fruit or fruit extracts in the mash, boil, primary or secondary fermentation.

Gluten-free
Brewed without ingredients containing gluten, i.e. barley, wheat, spelt, oats, rye or their derivatives. The ABV ranges can vary. UK definition: gluten content less than 20 parts per million (20 ppm).

Herb and spice
Any beer made with the addition of ingredients such as heather, ginger or certain vegetables – aromas and palate are determined by the type of adjunct used. The ABV ranges can vary.

Honey
Any cold- or warm-fermented beer made with the addition of honey – aromas and palate are determined by the type of adjunct used. The ABV ranges can vary.

Kriek/framboise
Cherry-flavoured beer with oud bruin base, featuring tart, slightly acidic notes plus earthy 'horse-blanket' character; some will be sweeter than others. Some variants use raspberries.

Low carb
Lagers that have been specifically brewed to have a low carbohydrate content. The ABV ranges can vary.

No alcohol (0 per cent)
No/very low alcohol, less than 0.5 per cent ABV.

Pumpkin beer

Popular with brewers in the USA, such beer uses pumpkins as an adjunct in the mash, boil, primary or secondary fermentation.

Rice

Cold fermented and brewed with a high proportion of rice. The ABV ranges can vary.

Rye beer

Rye beer, known as roggenbier in Germany, is brewed with a proportion of rye malt. Usually dark in colour and low in hops, the beer has spicy and fruit flavours. The taste of the rye often is present in the finished beer.

Sake-yeast beer

A beer brewed with sake yeast. The colour will depend on the malts used. Sake yeast, which can be slow to ferment, often produces strawberry or melon esters. The challenge for the brewer is to find a hop cocktail that can harmonise with the fruitiness.

Smoked

Any cold- or warm-fermented beer. Lagers are associated with the Bamberg region of Germany, using malt kilned over beechwood fires. Intense smoky aroma and a palate balanced by grassy hops. Long, refreshing finish with smoky malt, hop bitterness and light fruit.

Steam

A hybrid beer with elements of both lager and ale in its character, usually achieved by brewing lager yeasts at ale fermentation temperatures. Highly effervescent. The ABV ranges can vary.

Wood- and barrel-aged beer

A wood- or barrel-aged beer is one that has been aged for a period of time in a wooden barrel or in contact with wood. This beer is aged with the intention of imparting the particularly unique character of the wood and/or what has previously been in the barrel. New wood is likely to add vanilla flavours. Used sherry, rum, whisky casks or other barrels can be used, contributing to some unique and complex flavours.

A HISTORY OF BEER
IN HALF PINTS

We'll probably never know who the first people were to make and drink beer. But examples of making a drink with grain can be found since the beginning of recorded history. So what events led our ancestors to create a drink made from grains and water? Adding to this mixture the magic of yeast and a warming, life-enhancing food-rich drink was created.

As far as we can tell, about 9,000 or 10,000 years ago, somewhere in China or on the sweeping crescent-shaped fertile plains of Mesopotamia, nomadic hunters and gatherers started to grow and harvest an ancient form of grain. Limited archaeological evidence indicates these grains could have been used to make an early form of beer.

Some of our earliest evidence comes from pottery chips found in a Neolithic village at the Jiahu site in China, which contain traces of chemical compounds found in alcoholic drinks. Clay tablets from 4300 BC Babylonia have been found that detail recipes for an alcoholic drink made with grain. And archaeologists in China have discovered the residue of a 3,000-year-old millet drink, which was preserved inside a tightly sealed bronze vessel from a tomb in Anyang, the Shang Dynasty capital, in the fertile earth of the Yellow River valley.

It is likely that these ancient people made a drink that

was not just life-enhancing, but life-changing. The nomads gave up their lives of constant movement, following food and the seasons, and instead decided to establish permanent settlements near to their pastures. People were on the long and winding road to civilisation.

And what an excursion it has been. Beer has touched many areas of our history, laws, culture, science and technology. Our forebears' chance discovery that wetted grains could provide a nutritious drink has served us well.

An ancient oral poem from Babylonia called 'The Gilgamesh Epic' tells the story of the civilising influence of drinking beer. The ancient fable tells the story of Enkidu, a shaggy, unkempt beast of a man who, after spending a week with a woman, was taught to eat bread and drink beer … after that, he washed and became civilised.

The Ancient Egyptians drank beer, regarding it as one of life's essential pleasures. And there is plenty of evidence to show that they made an intoxicating drink from grains, which was used to honour the dead. In Ancient Egypt beer was the drink of the people. In the tombs of pharaohs, wine was given as offerings to the gods; beer was left in the tombs as sustenance for their servants' journeys to the next life. But beer wasn't just for the afterlife: Egyptian households were home to simple brewing equipment. Beer was the drink of the people, a staple, a liquid form of bread.

In Japan communities made a drink fermented from rice grains. According to tradition it was a drink of the imperial palaces and was drunk to bring people closer to the gods. The drink, similar to something we call sake today, would have seen communities chewing a mixture of rice and nuts, which was then spat into a large storage vessel. The sake produced was called *'kuchikami no sake'*, which means 'chewing the mouth sake'. According to some accounts, which probably aren't untrue, the chewing was always undertaken by virgins who were about to get married.

A similar method was used in Central and South America to make a drink called chicha – a mix of maize, peppercorns and local fruit. Enzymes in the saliva break down the starch in the maize to release the sugars necessary for fermentation, also the chewing would have helped to sterilise the sugars in the resultant gloop, stopping it being spoiled by wild yeasts and bacteria.

And throughout Africa archaeological evidence indicates beers were made from millet or sorghum, one of the oldest grains still used for beer making. Such a beer is still made today – often known as Chibiku or Shake Shake. Sold fresh, in waxed paper containers, it normally has to be shaken before being drunk, to restore its grainy, off-yoghurt consistency. According to local lore, in older times such drinks would come from supplies kept in large communal pots.

We don't know when brewing began in the British Isles, but according to two Irish archaeologists, Billy Quinn and Declan Moore, some of the most common archaeological monuments dating from Bronze Age Ireland, more than 4,000 years ago, were used for brewing. These monuments, known as *'fulacht fiadh'*, of which more than 4,500 are known to exist, are thought to have many uses, one of which could have been to make an ancient ale.

By AD 500 the Angles and Saxons had begun to arrive in Britain, to conquer and settle. Much of their social life revolved around beer and the ale house, and it seems they had developed the technology to build large hooped casks for carrying ale.

Some of the first evidence of brewing in Britain comes from strips of wood found by archaeologists in the 1980s, which had been left by Romans retreating from an exposed fort in

Northumbria. On the slivers of wood was writing, probably created sometime between AD 90 and 130 – a request from the fort's soldiers for more beer to be sent as supplies for the troops were running low. Known as the Vindolanda tablets, one contains the name Atrectus, who is believed to be the first named brewer in British brewing history.

By 770 Charlemagne was appointing brewers. Brewing was already taking place in what were to become some of the world's great brewing locations: Pilsen in Bohemia, Bavaria in Germany, Leuven in Belgium and Burton on Trent in England.

The church also played an important role in people's drinking lives. It was common for large religious houses to brew beer and set aside rooms where travellers and visitors could enjoy it. Across temperate Europe, brewing was increasing. Within decades of the start of the 7th century, brewing was underway at two monasteries in Germany: Kloster Weltenburg and Kloster Weihenstephan, with both claiming to be the oldest site for continuous brewing in the world. Outside the monasteries most brewing was done by women, who were known as brewsters. Indeed, women would be the principal brewers of beer for centuries until the industrialisation of the brewing process, which saw men take on the role.

Ale houses in England had become commonplace by the 9th century, with the ale brewed on the premises. These buildings were identified by long poles, and if they sold wine a bush of evergreens was hung as well.

In Bavaria, in 1516, the so-called Beer Purity Law (Reinheitsgebot) was established. It said that barley, hops and pure water were the only ingredients to be allowed in the brewing process. It didn't extend to the rest of Germany until 1906.

And by 1587, the first beer was being brewed by colonists in Virginia, but that didn't stop them sending back to England for more. America's first commercial brewery opened in Lower Manhattan in 1632; it was owned by the Dutch East India Company.

By the end of the 19th century, Burton on Trent in England had become the brewing capital of Britain, with a worldwide reputation. Its brewing origins stretched back to 1004 when monks at a Benedictine abbey brewed there. The water in the area was ideal for brewing ale-style beers. The water is very hard, meaning it is high in gypsum. This makes it easier to produce clear, golden ales with a high hop bitterness. Over time Burton became renowned for its golden ales. The opening of the canals at the end of the 18th century allowed the town's reputation and its beers to be carried far and wide, not just in England but to the four corners of what became the British Empire. By the end of the 19th century the town had between 20 and 30 large commercial breweries, including Bass and Marston's, whose beers can still be bought today.

Brewing in the town of Pilsen, in what is now called the Czech Republic, has a long history, but it is its clear, golden beer, first brewed in 1842, that has sealed the town's fame in brewing history. The term pilsner original meant 'from Pilsen'. Golden beers were not new; they were already brewed in Britain and Bavaria. It is now probably the most popular beer style in the world and is brewed just about everywhere: the template for mass-produced pale lagers.

Bavaria, in what is now southern Germany, is another important brewing region. Its brewers claim it is the undisputed cradle of the world's lager beer culture. Munich, the capital of Bavaria, was known to have brewing in 1269. Brewing thrived in the city because it is in one of the best barley-growing areas in Europe as well as next to Hallertau, a famed hop-growing area. Its contribution to beer culture is the annual Oktoberfest, first held in 1810; it confusingly takes place in the last two weeks of September and the first week of October. Only beers from the city's large breweries are served at the festival.

By 1876 the brewing industry as we understand it today was evolving. Louis Pasteur was able to describe scientifically the mysterious world of yeast. Modern brewing techniques were replacing those from the Middle Ages. Science, refrigeration and bottling were becoming widespread and took beer all over the world.

SOME OF THE BEST-KNOWN BEERS IN THE WORLD

There cannot be many countries left in the world where beer is not drunk or brewed. Beer is indeed a world drink and most of it is made by a few brewers. The brands they make are widely known and are drunk by millions of people every day. As a general rule they are pale lager-style beers, lacking in body and without much hop character or aroma. And despite the worldwide explosion of beers from new brewers or even old-style traditional brewers, the beers from these international breweries dominate beer sales.

The USA now has more than 3,000 brewers; in the 1980s, it was predicted that this number would be about 100. Anheuser-Busch (AB) InBev, which produces Budweiser, Coors and Miller, by far the biggest brewer. Light American lagers dominate the market, with the top sellers being Bud Light, Budweiser, Coors Light, Miller Lite and Michelob. Other big-selling brews include Pabst, Schlitz and Lone Star – it's not for nothing that these beers are often described as grass-cutting beers. Packed high and sold cheap in liquor stores, they are refreshing, thirst-quenching, unchallenging and a livener on a hot day after a bit of exercise.

In Argentina most locals drink Quilmes; travel to Brazil and people will be downing Skol or Brahma. In Chile and Peru they will be drinking Cristal, in Bolivia Pacena and in Ecuador Pilsener. The Colombians like to open a Poker, but you'll have to cross the border to Venezuela for a Polar. Go north to Mexico and Corona Extra is the beer of choice for many, while Jamaicans drink Red Stripe. Travel up to Canada and Budweiser is usually the beer people reach for first.

In Europe, a Danish favourite that is known worldwide, Carlsberg, was first brewed in 1847, and it is now a beer sold on most continents. The creator of the beer is the famed J. C. Jacobsen, who was renowned for his research into brewing and yeast technology. According to brewing legend, he smuggled the yeast used to brew the clear, golden Carlsberg from what is now the Czech Republic in a container stored in the top hat he wore on his head.

Heineken is much more than a Dutch institution. The Heineken family bought the Haystack brewery is 1864. It is now Europe's largest beer brand, operating in more than 170 countries and owning more than 120 breweries in at least 70 countries. Heineken also owns the other Dutch favourite, Amstel.

Germany is a renowned brewing nation – it still has more than 1,000 breweries. But most drinkers are content to drink local beers. Internationally, the best-known brand is Beck's, one of the family of beers produced by the world's biggest brewer, Anheuser-Busch InBev.

Holsten is another well-known brand which is part of Carlsberg. Internationally known, it is not the best-selling beer in Germany; some of the best-selling beers on the German market include Erdinger, Krombacher, Veltins, Warsteiner and Bitburger.

The United Kingdom now has more than 1,500 breweries. The country's top-selling lager is Carling, which is owned by Molson Coors. Other big-selling lagers are Fosters, Kronenbourg and Stella (which is brewed in Magor in South Wales). Popular lagers include Heineken, Carlsberg, Beck's and Grolsch. The country's best-selling ale brands are John Smith's, Boddington's and Guinness. Guinness is brewed in more than 40 countries. Drinkers in Ireland and Britain normally see it sold on draught. However, in many parts of the world, including Nigeria and Indonesia, it is sold in bottles in a variety of different strengths from 4.1 to 8 per cent ABV. Other best-selling ales include Greene King IPA, Greene King Speckled Hen, Sharp's Doom Bar and Fuller's London Pride.

With Abbey Ales, lambics, geuze and krieks, Belgium has a bewildering choice of beer styles, given the size of the country, and regional variations. Outside the country its best-known international beer brand is Stella Artois, but in the country itself more Jupiler is probably drunk. Leffe is another popular beer range.

The Czech Republic is one of the world's great brewing nations. Its modern-day reputation stems from 1842, when a golden lager named pilsner was developed. The country's biggest brand is Gambrinius. It's a national treasure and is revered by many Czech drinkers but is not very well known beyond the country's borders. Pilsner Urquell is also popular, as is Budvar. Many prefer to drink regional brands such as Staropramen (Prague) and Zatec (Zatec) rather than national ones.

Italy now has more than 700 brewers. Peroni and Moretti are probably the most popular beers, which are owned by international giants SABMiller and Heineken respectively. The Austrians like their Stiegel, Poles choose Tyskie and the Hungarians drink Borsodi. In Spain, Cruzcampo is a favourite partner with plates of tapas, while the Portuguese drink Sagres. Holidaymakers in Greece slake their thirst with Mythos, while in Turkey Efes is usually the drink of choice.

Travel to Russia and many choose Baltika. China is the

biggest beer market in the world and Snow, Tsingtao and Yanjing are widely available. In India, many will quench their thirst with a Kingfisher. The Thais have Chang and Singha, the Cambodians Ganzberg, Indonesians Bingtang and in Malaysia and Singapore many choose Tiger. In Laos Beerlao is the top seller, in the Philippines San Miguel tops the charts and South Koreans choose Cass.

Travel to Australia and the locals' preferred beer isn't Fosters, but rather Victoria Bitter (VB), whereas in New Zealand, Lion Red is the beer of choice. In Japan, Asahi is the most popular beer.

In Africa, the Algerians like to Tango, the Moroccan's fly the Flag, while Egyptians sup Stella. Others follow the Star to Nigeria, while in Namibia it would be rude not to drink a Windhoek. In Mozambique people choose Laurentina. Kenyans choose Tusker. In South Africa a BBQ would be incomplete without a Carling Black Label or a Castle.

WORLD'S TOP 10 SELLING BEERS

BEER	COUNTRY	OWNER
Snow	China	SABMiller/China Resource Enterprises
Tsingtao	China	Tsingtao
Budweiser	USA	AB-InBev
Yanjing Beer	China	Yanjing
Bud Light	USA	AB InBev
Corona Light	Mexico	AB InBev
Skol	Brazil	Carlsberg
Heineken	Netherlands	Heineken
Coors Light	USA	Molson Coors
Brahma	Brazil	AB InBev

THE MODERN
BREWING INDUSTRY

The pace of change in the modern brewing industry is breath-taking. New breweries – often described as craft breweries – open almost every day, while the large, transnational companies are growing through consolidation and acquisition.

It looks highly likely that there'll be a tie-up between the world's two largest brewers: Anheuser-Busch (AB) InBev made a takeover bid for SABMiller. AB InBev's brands include Budweiser, Stella Artois and Corona, while SABMiller owns Meantime, Peroni and Grolsch. If the deal is successful, the merged company would produce one-third of the world's beer. And already it looks like some of its brands will have to be sold off to appease competition authorities around the world.

Grolsch, Peroni and Meantime are reported to be up for grabs, with Japanese brewer Asahi said to be interested in buying the beers. However, if the deal does go ahead, the merged company would be likely to move aggressively into faster growing markets.

AB InBev has an eye on the African markets, where SABMiller dominates in 15 countries, and has a presence in a further 21. A merger would also strengthen its grip on South America and Mexico, which are by far its most profitable beer markets in the world.

However, the big conglomerates are also buying up some of the new craft brewers. AB InBev has recently agreed to buy the Breckenridge Brewery, adding a seventh US craft brewer to a portfolio that already includes Goose Island, Four Peaks, Blue Point and Elysian. The company also recently bought the Camden Town Brewery in London.

GLOBAL MARKET SHARE OF THE FIVE BIGGEST BEER COMPANIES

Anheuser-Busch InBev	20.8%
SABMiller	9.7%
Heineken	9.1%
Carlsberg	6.1%
China Resources Enterprise	6%

Source: Euromonitor, based on 2014 figures

THE 50 GREATEST
BEERS IN THE WORLD

50. TIPOPILS
Style: Pilsner
Strength: 5.2% ABV
Brewer: Birrificio Italiano
Country of origin: Italy
First brewed: 1996

Can there be a better looking beer? It's true we really do drink with our eyes. The body of the beer is golden sun shining in the glass and it is topped with a bold white head, as attractive as freshly fallen winter snow on the Italian Alps that surround the brewery.

When the first, golden-style beers were developed by Bavarian Josef Groll in the 1840s in the town of Pilsen, they were a revelation. And while a brewer gets the credit for this beer style, it was developments in malting technology and the serendipity of its location that enabled the beer to be served crystal-clear instead of murky.

As part of the transformational malting process, which releases the essential sugars the brewer needs, the grains have to be dried using heat from a fire. However, for many years maltsters couldn't control the furnaces' fervour and the malt would be burnt, dark and black – sending up in smoke the vital brewing sugars. The resultant dark grains of malt produced dark, often cloudy beer. Mastering the skill of controlling the heat not only saved brewers money but enabled the creation of clear, golden beers.

Groll's fortune was that his malt was dried in a kiln, imported or copied from England, that was fired not by direct heat from a wood fire, but by easily controllable indirect heat from a coke burner. It was this innovation that had led to England's legendary clear, golden pale ales using lighter coloured malt.

Another stroke of good fortune was the use of malt made from two-row spring barley, grown in Moravia and Bohemia (then part of the Austro-Hungarian Empire but now in the Czech Republic). Groll's maltster used a variety known as Hana. Nitrate, found naturally in grain, makes beer cloudy. Bohemian and Moravian barley is very low in nitrates, making it easier to brew crystal-clear, eye-entrancing beers. The mother and father of modern varieties, it is not grown today. But the malt had two other attributes that made it ideal for brewers: it helps make beer with a good mouthfeel, a tactile sensation on the tongue that makes you want to have a second sip, and it also helps create a fulsome, foaming, head that makes it look good in the glass.

Lastly, Groll had access to soft water. Arguably water is the most important ingredient: it certainly makes up more than 85 per cent of most beers. The yeast strain used to ferment the malt thrives in the soft water of the area around the town of Pilsen. Today brewers understand the science and chemistry of water and can adjust it, a process often called Burtonisation, to make it as hard or soft as they need.

A pioneer of the craft brewing scene in Italy, the brewery's founder Agostino Arioli started to brew at home while he was still at school. But it was a trip to Granville Island Brewery in Vancouver, Canada, that opened his eyes to the potential for great beer – and the need for technology and artistry to be partners in the brewing process. On his return to his homeland, Agostino decided a schoolboy dream should become an adult reality and he established the Birrificio Italiano brewpub in Marione near Lake Como, with his brother Stefano and some friends.

He had always been an admirer of pilsen-style beers and his ambition was to brew the best. Agostino is meticulous in his approach to brewing. He visited farms to see the ingredients growing. He likes to taste everything. He wants to understand the contribution of every ingredient to the beer he makes. He's even been known to drive to Bavaria to pick the hops he wants for his beers.

He doesn't like to rush the production process and believes that by taking time he will draw flavours of great depth and complexity from the ingredients. Too many so-called pilsen-style beers have been made by cutting corners – scrimping on time and the ingredients. This produces pallid, thin, often sweet beers with little depth of character.

Tipopils is dry to taste. The golden beer swirls, with floral, grassy hop flavours and a hint of honey. Its finish is refreshing, with a pleasing, long, lingering bitterness. And it is easy to appreciate why it is regarded as one of the best craft pilsners in the world.

It's a great beer to drink with food – and it also great to drink between meals too.

49. ANGRY BOY BROWN ALE
Style: American brown ale
Strength: 7% ABV
Brewer: Baird Brewing
Country of origin: Japan
First brewed: 2001

In the land of the rising sun, people like to drink beer. Brewing beer probably began in Japan sometime in the 1870s; clearly many took to it, as more than a century later consumption has risen to 40 litres per person every year.

Japan's brewers are no slouches when it comes to producing beer: they make more than 15 million hectolitres (hl) of beer a year. To put that in perspective, Belgium's brewers produce around 18 million hl every year.

Most of Japan's output comes from large industrial brewers. They make drinkable, but probably not memorable, beers. Beyond Japan, it wasn't until the 1990s that many people heard about Japanese brewers. Then there came ice beers, which saw the big brewers produce very clear, clean-tasting beers by freezing the beer; this removed some of the water and some impurities, leaving a slightly stronger drink. However, it was a change of licensing law that led to the development of a craft beer industry making interesting beers.

In 1994 the annual capacity requirement for a brewing licence in Japan was reduced from 2 million litres to just 60,000. This opened the door for a proliferation of small craft breweries. Today, there are more than 280 in the country.

One of the most interesting is Baird Brewing. American Bryan Baird and his wife Sayuri founded the Baird Brewery

© Baird Brewing

in 2001. It is now regarded as one of the best of the country's craft brewers and produces flavoursome beers drawing on the traditions of American craft brewers.

An American brown ale draws its taste roots from Britain, but US brewers just make them bigger. In England in the 1700s most ales would have been as brown ales. Beer in which dark malts and caramel predominate, lightly hopped and shy; the Americans of course added more hops. Baird likes his beer to have personality. It's the distinguishing feature between them and industrial beers, he says.

Angry Boy pours a light red brown into a glass. It is a beer that deceives. Its quiet demeanour hides an angry Samurai. The beer has complexity, a barely controlled bitterness. The whole hops deliver a spicy aura, and a long spicy finish. Underneath is a long, fruit caramel, sweet finish as one would expect from a brown ale. The addition of some Japanese sugars delivers comforting caramel notes. A cocktail of whole hop flower cones gives the beer an earthy, spicy distinction.

Bryan Baird said: 'Growing the market larger is a matter of more beer meeting the high standards of Japanese consumers as well as more educational efforts aimed at deepening consumer understanding of beer history and tradition. Our beer is unfiltered, secondarily fermented in the package and thus naturally carbonated. We exclusively use whole flower hops. In production, we aim to process beer is as simple and minimalist a way as possible. We aim for beers of character which we define as: Character = Balance + Complexity.'

It's a curious beer, something of a Jekyll and Hyde. There is an interplay not between good and evil but glorious hops and caramel, malt sweetness. Easy to drink, but be cautious: at 7 per cent its alcoholic strength could catch you out.

Anger is energy. Use it, then let it go.

48. FARO
Style: Faro
Strength: 4.5% ABV
Brewer: Lindemans
Country of origin: Belgium
First brewed: 1978

If spontaneously fermented lambics are rare, then faros are even more so. Like true lambics, they are from the Payottenland region of Brussels, Belgium, which is also known as the Senne Valley. A faro is a sweetened lambic – sugar is added to soften the sharp, acerbic acidity of a lambic.

The style was widely available until the early part of the 20th century, but then drinkers fell out of love with it and turned to mainstream lager styles for refreshment. Like many of the makers of faro, the brewer Lindemans stopped producing it when demand fell. However, in 1978 it decided to revive it. Across the Atlantic in America, a new and developing beer culture was evolving. People were eager to discover and try long-lost brews such as faro and Lindemans thought there would be an opportunity to export the beer.

The beer was traditionally made with weaker runnings from the mash or lauter tun, which is essentially a large sieve to separate spent grains from the sweet wort. At the end of mashing as the liquid is drained out, it is rinsed with warm water. The first runnings produce a sweet wort. However, there still could be some fermentable material left in the grain, so similar to using a teabag for a second or even a third time, warm water is run through the mash again, producing a lighter, less sweet liquid.

© Lindemans

Faros are typically weaker than a lambic. Traditionally they might have been served at 2–3 per cent ABV, which means they would be very susceptible to bacterial infection and turning into vinegar, and would probably have been drunk very fresh to try to avoid this. However, modern versions are normally between 4 and 5 per cent ABV. Originally, without the body or acidic intensity of a lambic, brewers would often use a sugar or even some malt to sweeten the beer and add some body. The sugar, no doubt, might have masked any bacterial infection the beer might have had.

The base beer for a faro is spontaneously fermented: the process is similar to making natural wines in which no yeast is added. Once fermented, Lindemans' Faro is left to mature in an oak barrel for a year, before liquid brown candy sugar is added and it is bottled. The beer is pasteurised to stop it re-fermenting.

Some brewers would have also added herbs, spices and fruit, including coriander and orange peel. Perhaps these were early examples of what became known as Belgian wit beers.

Often served on draught, sweetness could be added in a pub or bar as the beer is served or in the brewery. A similar technique can still be found in Germany in bars selling Berliner weisse.

Faros are sweeter beers that lack the intensity of a lambic; the demand for them is very small, which makes them worth seeking out in the interest of satisfying one's beer-hunting curiosity.

They are rustic beers – made for refreshment – similar in their own way to a farmhouse cider. They were beers for consuming in large quantities – a glass of faro was liquid, sweet bread, intended to refresh a worker after a day's labour in the fields.

Indeed, when Lindemans first began to brew in 1822, it was a small farmhouse brewery supplying beer for local farmworkers. Today, the brewery is still owned by the same family, but people's tastes have changed and its brew house is modern and much of its output is exported to the USA.

According to Lindemans, the 16th-century artist Pieter Bruegel, who painted many rural scenes of Flemish life showing people drinking beer, was inspired by faro and without it 'he would have remained an ordinary amateur painter whose canvases couldn't even have been sold at a flea market'.

Amber to the eye, with a vibrant white head, Lindemans' Faro sees candy sweetness and bitterness vying for attention. Its attributes are similar to a sweetish sherry. Its aroma is sweet and caramel. It lacks the acidic, vinous complexity of a lambic but does have hints of marmalade, brown sugar, citrus and sherbet. Fruit and caramel aroma, balanced by subtle complexity and refreshing acidity. The flavour starts sweet, with suggestions of brown sugar or orange marmalade, and finishes with crisp tartness.

It is said the beer is the favourite of many amateur cyclists, who rather than reaching for a sweet, sugary energy drink after a day's exertion in the saddle will search for their bottle opener and drink a Faro.

In Belgium the art of pairing beer with food has been taken to new heights and many chefs like to pair a Faro with pork or fish dishes or recommend it as a palate-cleansing aperitif.

47. GEUZE MARIAGE PARFAIT
Style: Geuze
Strength: 8.8% ABV
Brewer: Boon
Country of origin: Belgium
First brewed: 1975

In 1975, at a time when many brewers and blenders in Flanders were giving up the art and craft of making the region's iconic geuze and kriek beers, the young Frank Boon decided he would take over the sour beer brewery run by René de Vits, who was going to retire and close the business because he had no children to pass the brewery on to.

Brewing is thought to have taken place on this site in the village of Lembeek, on the banks of the River Senne, since sometime around 1680, but it came into the hands of the de Vits family in 1927. It is thought that the village may have given its name to the lambic beer style. Frank Boon's passion is lambic beers, which are fermented by wild airborne yeasts found in the Payottenland region of Flanders. His geuze is a blend of young and old lambics that produces a sparkling, refreshing beer. Traditionally, many makers of geuze were not brewers but independent blenders, who would buy in the beers as and when they needed them.

Boon is often credited with being responsible for lambic beer's recent revival. At his brewery, which moved to its current site in the centre of Lembeek in 1986, there are many large wooden casks called foeders. Here the beers are matured, with their complex tastes developing through contact with the inside of the barrel and the air that comes in through the pores in the wood.

Sometimes pronounced 'goose', but more often 'gur-zah', the beers are usually sold in a corked and wire-caged bottle. Often these beers are described as the champagne of beers. The young lambic from which it is blended will still have some residual unfermented sugar in it. This means a secondary fermentation will take place in the bottle: it won't create much more alcohol, but it will build up a lot of carbonation in the beer, or in other words a lot of bubbles.

The older lambic will be rich in *Brettanomyces*, which is commonly called Brett. Brett is a strain of yeast; often thought of as a wild yeast, it is these days carefully cultured. It creates weird, funky flavours, which can often be found with beers stored in wood for a long time. Typically, a Brett beer will have flavours of horse blanket, farmyard or even earth. These flavours are shunned by winemakers and are often regarded as major faults, but to brewers and blenders like Frank Boon they add a new, intense dimension to the flavour and character of beer.

The name *Brettanomyces* literally means the British yeast. It is often found in what was known as stock ale, a term probably from sometime around 1700, which referred to a strong brew left to mature for a long time. During this time unknown elements of the yeast would often start a third, or tertiary, fermentation, which created not sour flavours but a crisp acidity and a tongue-sucking dryness.

The Geuze Mariage Parfait, at 8 per cent ABV, is a soaring harmonious duet of a three-year-old lambic that has been quietly and gently maturing in one of the 230 large oak vats blended with younger, more vivacious lambics, filtered and aged in a wire-corked bottle for at least six months. The skill of lambic and geuze brewers is much more than managing fermentation; the management of wood and blending is

© Boon

equally if not more important. Just as with whisky or wine blending, each barrel has its own character and the skill of the blender is recognising and managing this. The artful blender needs to know which barrels to use and which need to be left in the cellar to mature for longer.

The Parfait blend consists of 95 per cent old lambic and 5 per cent young. The beers are blended together and filtered, chilled and bottled. The bottles are then placed in a cellar at fermentation temperature so the secondary fermentation can take place. This is followed by a minimum six-month fermentation at low temperatures. The resultant hand-crafted beer is an intense entrancing concord of smooth and bitter flavours with layers of vanilla from the oak barrels and a tongue-tingling bitter clove finish. A beer of such sublime passion deserves to be enjoyed with fine rich food. Try it with a goat's cheese drizzled with olive oil and dressed with some fresh herbs, or even a plate of snails that have been cooked in a stock containing a dash of the beer.

The beer will store for many years in the bottle – and it is said if a drinker ever wants to know its bottling date, they should subtract twenty years from the 'best before' date printed on the label.

46. CENTENNIAL IPA
Style: American IPA
Strength: 7.2% ABV
Brewer: Founders
Country of origin: USA
First brewed: 2001

American brewers like to take big European beer styles and make them even bigger. And so it is with India pale ales (IPA). An English ale style, they tend to be strongish, usually above 5 per cent ABV and well hopped by European standards. A US version is likely to be even stronger and have loads more hops and has become recognised as a beer style in its own right, the American IPA.

Flower, citrus and pine aromas exude from Centennial. This is a big rock 'n' roll beer with the volume turned up to 11. Indeed, it's a remarkable beer, which rightly should be in most beer drinkers' top 50.

The new-wave American brewers' beers are dominated by aromatic hop flavours. And Centennial is one of the trinity of the three C hops that includes Cascade and Columbus, which are the hops of choice for many US craft brewers.

Centennial hops are often dubbed the super Cascade, but in truth their citrus aromas are not as heavy and overpowering as Cascade. Many beers are made with a cocktail of hops, but not so with this Founders' beer. The beer's name gives it away, it is just made with one single hop variety, Centennial. But the brewer uses the hop intelligently. Hops are added throughout the wort boiling process, but this can destroy many of the hops' volatile oils. To avoid this, brewers dry hop, a cold infusion after fermentation, which adds and

© Founders

intensifies hop aromas. And the new wave of American craft brewers who were starved of hop flavours in domestic brews went about dry hopping with particular fervour.

However, there is much more to dry hopping than just adding in handfuls of hop flowers or pellets. A careful balance between malt and hops flavours is essential. Get it right and the result is a beautifully balanced and aromatic beer. Get it wrong and the beer can be oxidised, grassy and even vegetal. Well, Founders has got it right.

Amber in colour, Centennial IPA has an impressive driving bass and drum line from the barley malt, but it is the use of the hops that helps this beer to rise to impressive heights. It has soaring aromas of grapefruit and tangerine, marvellous fruity notes from the ale yeast and a big mouthfeel. This is a serious beer for grown-ups who want to take their time enjoying a beer. It's voluptuous and lip caressing, which gives way to a long, warming bitter finish.

The Michigan brewer was founded in 1997 by Mike Stevens and Dave Engbers. It bumbled along for a number of years, at first making beers without much distinction. But then, following a brush in 2001 with bankruptcy, caution was thrown to the wind. It was do (and succeed) or die. Out went the bland and in came big, bold flavours – which the founders of Founders say were the beers they wanted to drink. And customers shared their enthusiasm for these new unflinchingly complex beers – and Founders became one of the fastest growing brewers in America.

Centennial is almost tame when compared with other beers from the brewery's portfolio such as Breakfast Stout, which is infused with a swathe of coffee beans, or Backwoods Bastard, which has been aged in bourbon barrels. But that doesn't stop it standing out from the crowd.

Many brewers like to pair food with beer – and indeed

Centennial is an ideal partner with big fatty cheeses and meaty sandwiches, but the people at Founders always like to do things differently. They pair their beers with movies. The brewery's beer and film sommelier recommends a glass of Centennial should be supped while watching *The Big Lebowski*, a 1998 Coen brothers film about a likeable, unemployed, no-gooder known as the Dude, who spends his nights at the local bowling alley. The film is a typical Coen comedy and is a classic, just like Centennial.

45. BERLINER WEISSE
Style: Berliner weisse
Strength: 3% ABV
Brewer: New Glarus
Country of origin: USA
First brewed: 2015

Located in the small town of New Glarus in Wisconsin, a town with a proud Swiss heritage, the founders Dan and Deb Carey are renowned for their world-class interpretations of a wide variety of beer styles, mainly Belgian. However, it is a version of a German beer that merits inclusion.

Berliner weisse is a style that originates in and around Berlin. Its history is as turbid and cloudy as a glass of the beer. The beer's prime characteristics are a soft sourness, some fruity overtones and a bit of a haze. And its soft effervescence has seen it described as the champagne of the North.

The style evolved from sometime in the 17th century. It could have been influenced by émigrés from Flanders who

started to brew a light, easy-drinking, low in alcohol wheat beer. By the 19th century Berliner weisse, which had to be developed to have its distinctive tartness, was the drink of choice for people in the city, and Berlin boasted more than 700 breweries producing their own version.

It seems the beers were very pale, slightly hazy and carbonated, with a light sour tang from the presence of lactic acid bacteria. Often lacking in body, raspberry syrup or sweet woodruff would be added to them on serving to add complexity and to soften the tartness.

The beers were made with a mixture of 50 per cent wheat and 50 per cent barley, with low amounts of hops. After mashing the wort was not boiled with the hops as most brewers do. Instead, the hops were boiled separately in water. The wort and boiled infusion were blended together; the hot hopped water helped raise the temperature of the mash, drawing more of the fermentable sugars out of the cereal grains.

As the wort wasn't boiled, it was prone to infection from the surviving lactic acid bacteria. Add to this the fact that the wood in which the beer was fermented was also host to its own lactic bacteria and it becomes easier to understand how the beer's signature dry and slightly acidic character was achieved. This was not the same as the sourness created in Belgian-style lambics, which came from spontaneous fermentation. As with most other beers, a brewer put yeast into Berliner weisse. However, tastes changed and the style all but died out in the 20th century, except for a very small output from two breweries in Berlin.

It was left to some of the new wave of American craft brewers to create their own versions of the style, which probably saved it from extinction. New Glarus's version of a Berliner weisse was brewed as part of its Thumbprint series, brewed for uber beer geeks. The beers are brewed in small batches and many have been one-offs. However, popular styles have been known to make a comeback.

The Glarus variant of the style has sparkling, fresh, entrancing flavours. Riesling grapes and Wisconsin White Wheat are barrel fermented with five yeasts and the living beer is put into a bottle.

In a glass, the beer looks a hazy gold and its aroma is tart and lemony. Its bubbles caress the tongue and it has a sparkling finish. The grapes add a green tartness to this complex, refreshing beer. Brewed for the summer season, it's a great refresher and the perfect drink to sip and celebrate the hot sun slipping below the horizon.

So to paraphrase the title of Christopher Isherwood's classic novel of life in Berlin in the early 1930s, which became the award winning musical *Cabaret*, let's not say Goodbye to Berliner Weisse.

44. WHITE
Style: Belgian white
Strength: 5.1% ABV
Brewer: Allagash
Country of origin: USA
First brewed: 1995

Time changes people's perceptions of a beer. When Allagash's founder Rob Tod first made his White, people asked him why it wasn't more accessible and told him to get rid of the spices and the wheat. Thankfully, he didn't listen to any of them. Now it's his best-selling beer. The customer isn't always right.

Tod was inspired to brew the beer having heard of the work of Pierre Celis, a Belgian who single-handedly revived his country's classic style of wheat beer. In 1965, Celis, a former milkman, decided to brew a beer in his hay loft in Hoegaarden, Flanders that was like the beer of his youth. He used the traditional ingredients for a white beer of water, yeast, raw wheat, malted barley hops, coriander seed and dried curaçao orange peel to create Hoegaarden. And so was born modern Belgian white beer.

The beer quickly gained cult status, especially among younger drinkers. In the 1980s, with demand for the product continuing to grow, Celis bought a local soft drinks factory that he turned into a brewery. When fire destroyed the Hoegaarden brewery in 1985, Celis accepted financial help from Stella Artois and subsequently sold the brewery to its parent Interbrew in 1991. At the age of 65, he then established the Celis brewery in Austin, Texas, and with the help of his daughter Christine he continued making white beer to what he described as the original Hoegaarden recipe. Eventually the brewery was bought by Miller, who closed it in 2001.

Celis's white beer is regarded as the authentic Belgian wheat beer, top fermented and then re-fermented in the bottle. It has a distinctive hazy yellow colour, and an alcohol content of 5 per cent ABV. It is a sweet and sour beer with a little bitterness – slightly spicy, with a strong touch of coriander and a hint of orange. Celis's creation has been often mimicked but rarely bettered.

Allagash's version is a winner and has picked up multiple golds in the World Beer Cup and the Great American Beer Festival. It has the style's classic white cloudiness in the glass. Spicy on the nose, it has swathes of herbal, fruity citrus notes. It dances lightly on the tongue and it is full of crispy wheat flavours overlain with a hint of tartness and long, fruity citrus flavours.

Food pairing is a major part of Belgium's beer culture and it is something that brewer Tod was keen to do in the USA. Each year, the brewery holds a cooking contest at the Institute of Culinary Education in New York as a way to further the awareness of both pairing and cooking fine foods with beers. Allagash's White is a versatile food partner; light and refreshing, it pairs with a salad. But the beer also has an inner strength, making it a weighty companion to a spicy seafood stew. The beer also works well with the spicy sweetness of Thai food – lemongrass, ginger and sugar are its culinary soulmates.

Tod has also taken his love of everything Belgian to a new level by building his own coolship, an open vessel that exposes unfermented beer to the air. He says brewing Belgian style encourages experimentation. After the mashing, the liquid is transferred into the vessel. During the cooling process, naturally wild yeasts inoculate the wort. In the morning it is transferred into French oak wine barrels, where the entire fermentation and ageing process takes place, and can take anything from one to three years. It is a process more likely to be found in the Senne Valley in Belgium where it is used by brewers of lambic beers, than in Portland, Maine.

43. PALE ALE (AMARILLO)
Style: Ale
Strength: 5.7% ABV
Brewer: The Kernel
Country of origin: UK
First brewed: 2010

Pale ale, it's just an ordinary, copper-coloured, bitter beer, isn't it?

There is nothing ordinary about any of the beers from The Kernel. Bland is probably not a word that is in the repertoire of Evin O'Riordan, who founded The Kernel Brewery at Tower Bridge, London, in a railway arch in 2010. He is adamant that he wants to make beers that force people to confront and consider what they are drinking. And he makes pale ales that are complex and, some might say, confrontational. His stout and porters are big; he has experimented with conditioning beer in wine barrels and he has even tried raspberry sour.

It was a trip to New York that opened his eyes to the potential of beer. He was in the city to learn about another member of the fermented family, cheese. He had worked for many years as a cheese seller, but in New York it was beer not cheese that stole his heart and soul. He came across brewers making beers that were no pale imitations of British ales. Many of the new wave of US craft brewers were exploring the possibilities that the new and rediscovered varieties of hops, with their big, bold fruit flavours, brought to beer.

He returned to London, determined to learn how to brew interesting beers. He might be self-taught, but in two years it was a hobby that became a business. He has also developed his own distinctive but minimalist packaging design. He wants the beer to do the talking. He is a huge fan of American beers and their use of big, bold fruit-flavoured hops and it is these he manages with exquisite skill. With innate precision, he understands how these flavours will work in his thought-provoking creations.

The Kernel has been at the forefront of London's recent beer renaissance and this is in no small part down to O'Riordan's willingness to share and collaborate, which has helped bring beer to a new audience. For, in a few short years, he and his brewing team have created some of the most stunning beers in the country and restored London as a powerhouse of creative brewing.

Part of his recipe for success is built around a heartfelt belief that he should work with other brewers to produce new beers or historical recreations. Taste and creativity, not the watchwords of an accountant or a marketing executive intent only on profit, decide what is put into a mash tun. It is almost as if he treats each batch of beer he brews as a work of art and he is striving to achieve perfection – using his palette of grain, hops and yeast.

Most brewers' ambition for their beers is that they should be consistent, so if they make a batch of bitter it should taste the same as the one that was made before, and the next one they make should taste the same as the one they've just made. But beer making isn't just a simple chemical process – the nuances of ingredients will change from harvest to harvest. O'Riordan's notion of consistency is that he wants each brew to be consistently excellent, accepting that it might vary in taste and character from a previous brew. His uncompromising quest for excellence has made his beers some of the country's most sought after. He is an adventurer inspired by London's historical beer styles. He is a particular

© The Kernel

fan of porters and stouts, and the rule-breaking creativity of the American craft beer revolution. One of his first beers was based on an 1890s recipe from the long-defunct Truman Brewery. He researched beers brewed by the Durden Park Beer Circle, a group of enthusiastic and skilled home brewers dedicated to recreating old beer styles.

He has probably used more types of malt and hops in the last twelve months than a brewer from a generation ago would have seen in a lifetime. Mosaic, Simcoe, Centennial, Summit, Citra and Nelson Sauvin are just some of the flavoursome hops recently used. His pale ales, IPAs, stouts and porters are constantly changing – each month there are different hops and alcoholic strengths.

The Pale Ale I tried was Amarillo. It's crisp, clean and sharp. The signature flavours of late addition Amarillo hops bring aromas of summer flowers, orange citrus zest and some pepper and spice. It's a beer to savour; a beer to have a conversation with.

42. TRIBUTE
Style: Ale
Strength: 4.2% ABV
Brewer: St Austell
Country of origin: UK
First brewed: 1999

Could this beer ever be eclipsed, would it be Daylight Robbery?

In the late 1990s, Roger Ryman was employed as a young assistant brewer at Maclays in the Scottish town of Alloa.

Here he was inspired by a new light, golden and hoppy IPA launched by rival brewer Caledonian under the name of Deuchars. At Harviestoun Brewery, a former Dagenham car salesman, Ken Brooker, was starting to produce some fresh golden ale with distinctive hop characteristics. One of the first to use imported hop varieties from the USA, he inspired Ryman to introduce the likes of Liberty, Mount Hood and Cascade hops into the range of seasonal beers brewed at Maclays.

In 1999, Ryman's career took him on a 600-mile journey to St Austell Brewery in Cornwall, where he was appointed head brewer. The board of St Austell had realised that they were facing some stiff competition, especially from a new beer called Doom Bar by the new Cornish microbrewer Sharp's. Ryman brought with him the creative ability to brew a new seasonal beer every two months: his first task was to produce something new. Given the entrenched and leaden conservatism of most traditional British ale brewers, this was indeed an inspired brief.

He was asked to brew a seasonal ale to mark the forthcoming solar eclipse. Ryman's predecessor Andrew McClure had already come up with a name for the beer, Daylight Robbery – but that was all. So on 11 August 1999, the date of the eclipse, when most of England seemed shrouded in cloud, the new beer was launched. Roger had shunned the idea of yet another brown bitter. So he produced a paler ale, underpinned by great depth and structure from Maris Otter barley. Ryman is a huge supporter of the attributes of this barley, which is shunned by many agri-economists and brewers. He said: 'When Maris Otter was introduced, the whole smell in the brewhouse at St Austell changed. Smell is supposedly one of the most effective stimulants of memory. The first brew with Maris Otter at St Austell took

me immediately back to the brew-house at Maclays. If barley variety can have such a dramatic effect on the aroma of the mash during brewing, then surely it must have an effect on the flavour of the finished beer?'

For the hops he turned away from the traditional English Fuggles and Golding because he wanted a beer that was moderately bitter and aromatic. So he chose the American hop Willamette and Styrian Golding from Slovenia.

Well, the day of the eclipse was probably not as spectacular as many had hoped, but it did thrust the beer into the limelight. Indeed, it went on to eclipse the sales of all other St Austell beers. The named had to be changed – marketing and sales thought a beer called Daylight Robbery sent out the wrong message. And so it became Tribute.

In an era of in-your-face aromatic hops, Willamette hops might seem somewhat staid. Citra, Simcoe and Mosaic hops might be considered to be sexier. But that doesn't stop the beer being a great example of a British pale ale – balanced, well constructed, relatively low in strength and full of flavour. The beer brought a very traditional family brewer into the 21st century, which is why Ryman was named by the British Guild of Beer Writers as its brewer of the year in 2006.

Ryman is also the founder of St Austell's annual Celtic Beer Festival: a boisterous carnival of great beers, held in the labyrinth of cellars and corridors underneath the brewery. In the vaults, over one weekend in November, the brewery rocks to loud music and beer. Here can be savoured not just brews from many of the region's other brewers but experimental brews produced by Ryman and his brewing team. Highlights have included a German-style wheat beer full of spice, apple and banana flavours, which has gone on to be a regular brew called Clouded Yellow; a tropical fruity Experimental 622 made with an unknown hop; the robust

Hopped Up Lager; a smooth 1913 Stout; and an authentic 14th-century ale called Gruitlyn's.

41. GAMMA RAY
Style: American pale ale
Strength: 5.4% ABV
Brewer: Beavertown
Country of origin: UK
First brewed: 2012

The idea was simple, to create a juicy, tropical, hop-forward beer. According to Beavertown's founder Logan Plant, Gamma Ray is a beer you can sit and drink all day, rammed with juicy malts and huge tropical aromas of mango and grapefruit. These bursts of tropical flavours come from the massive additions of whole-leaf Columbus, Bravo, Amarillo, Citra and Calypso hops that are added to the brew. The beer is then dry hopped for days, driving the punchy aromas that make it so distinctive.

The brewery journey began with Plant's experimentation as a home brewer. Inspired by brews across the world, Plant started experimenting using a 50-litre rice pan as a hot liquor tank, a camping cool box as a mash tun and a tea urn as a kettle. He soon discovered that he'd rather be a rock 'n' roll brewer than a rock 'n' roll star.

A plan was formed to open the brewery in the kitchen of a BBQ restaurant. And drawing on time spent in the USA, where the culture of pairing food and beer is well advanced, along came some great beers. Smog Rocket was paired with

© Beavertown

the spice and rub being used on the restaurant's pork ribs, and 8 Ball Rye IPA was paired with the smoked molasses and char of the beef ribs. And in homage to his youth, the original Neck Oil recipe was based around Plant's favourite best bitter from the Black Country in the West Midlands. And then came Gamma Ray – colleague Nick Dwyer came up with the name Gamma Ray and showed Plant a drawing of some spacemen on Mars firing lasers and being attacked by UFOs. Well, it's not quite Life on Mars, but it gives life to the beer.

The brewery grew too big to continue life in a pub's cellar and moved to Hackney Wick, and then that space became too small and the brewery moved to its current purpose-built home in Tottenham Hale. But no great beers are produced by one person – it is team work. In 2014 Jenn Merrick was appointed as head brewer.

A good brewer's beer started to reach great heights as Merrick used her skills to produce Beavertown's five core beers and undertook experiments with a new beer every few weeks through its Alpha Series range, using new yeasts. However, it was Gamma Ray that captured the attention of the judges at the International Beer Challenge and saw Merrick named brewer of the year by the British Guild of Beer Writers. According to the Beer Writers' citation, the thing that makes Merrick stand out 'is one of the hall marks of all good brewers through the ages, and now in an era when we define brewers by whether they are industrial or craft ... is that over and above their creative and scientific skills, it is their ability and desire to share, collaborate and experiment'. And what an experiment Gamma Ray is, and it is one that is being repeated on a regular basis.

Pale ales might be an English beer, but its child American pale ale is bigger than its father. What was commonplace over there is now over here. American pale ales evolved in the 1980s at the start of the country's microbrewing revival. Late hop additions in the brewing process define and embrace the character of an American pale ale. At first they showcased citrus and piney flavours. But then as brewers wanted to evolve even more flavoursome but drinkable beers, other flavours that had been ignored by brewers for a generation were rediscovered, including blackcurrant, pineapple and tropical.

The skill of making a great American pale ale comes in balancing the bitterness of the hops with the solid base of the malt; it's this that holds everything in place. The style is much more assertive than its English progenitor. It makes drinkers sit up and listen.

Gamma Ray's immense structure comes from a trio of malts – best pale, Caragold and Caramalt. The yeast's influence, other than creating the warming alcohol, is relatively restrained but brings with it some fruity, estery flavours. Beavertown's brewing team adds handfuls and handfuls of whole-leaf American hops at the end of the boil, giving huge hop flavours. The beer is then dry hopped for days, creating the luscious swathes of tropical fruit aromas – this is much more than a beer, it's a stairway to brewing and drinking heaven.

40. MACKESON STOUT

Style: Milk stout
Strength: 2.8% ABV
Brewer: Anheuser-Busch InBev
Country of origin: UK
First brewed: 1907

Some might regard this beer as a historical throwback – or a drink only fit for older people or nursing mothers. But there cannot be many other British beer brands that have a lineage going back more than 100 years. Mackeson Milk Stout first appeared early in the 20th century. The beer is a member of the porter and stout family, which was very popular at the time. A sweetish, dark beer, it was brewed by Mackeson of Hythe, Kent. The brewery owned the rights to a style of brewing that involved adding lactose sugar originally derived from milk to the beer. It called the beer a milk stout. By the standards of the time, it was not very strong at 3 per cent ABV.

The beer doesn't actually contain milk, but lactose can be derived from milk. The sugar in lactose is not fermented by the brewing yeast, but its importance is what it does to the beer. It adds a little sweetness, which probably masked some sourness in the base beer making it more palatable, and it gives it a fuller mouthfeel. The beer not only tastes better but it feels better. For good reason drinkers often described the beer's taste as being creamy.

It was a style that quickly gained in popularity and Mackeson had the commercial nous to license the brewing of the beer to other breweries. By the start of the First World

War in 1914, more than a dozen breweries were producing Mackeson Milk Stout.

As was common medical advice at the time, drinkers were told that the beer would give them energy and that it was ideal for nursing mothers and invalids. And one German doctor recommended that for health reasons drinkers should always choose beer over wine – and it was cheaper. The original Mackeson label bore the strapline 'Each pint contains the energising carbohydrates of ten ounces of pure dairy milk'.

The brewer's ownership changed a number of times and eventually it came under the ownership of Whitbread, which went on to be a national brewer. By the mid-1930s the beer was available nationally and in the portfolio of most breweries. Around this time the draught version was stopped, but it went on to be a great success as a bottled beer. However, after the end of the Second World War, in an era of rationing and austerity, British civil servants took a dim view that milk should be used in a beer and Whitbread simply changed the beer's name to Mackeson Stout.

The success of the bottled beer was indeed remarkable. By the end of the 1950s it was Whitbread's best seller, comprising nearly 50 per cent of the company's output. Today, we might think it unusual that so much bottled beer was sold in pubs. However, it makes sense when considering brewers couldn't refurbish their rundown pubs' cellars because the post-war government had diverted most available bricks and mortar into house building. The conditions for keeping draught beer had become very poor and it was easily spoiled.

By the 1960s, brewers were keen to establish and maintain national brands and television advertising on the new commercial channel was seen as key to a beer's success. Mackeson appeared on national television in

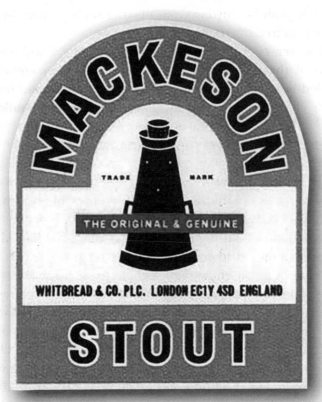

© Anheuser-Busch InBev

an advertisement that starred the famed actor Bernard Miles. It wasn't long before many people knew by heart the advertisement's catch line: 'Looks good, tastes good – and by golly it does you good'. Today, advertising regulations in the UK prohibit anyone from making such positive health assertions in advertisements for beer.

However, over time drinking trends changed and people tired of the beer – and they turned to lighter coloured, chilled beers sold on draught. The government had finally made changes so that pub owners could obtain the building materials needed to refurbish their cellars. The era of mass-produced chilled lagers sold in centrally heated pubs had begun in Britain.

Today, the output of the beer is miniscule – it's rarely found in pubs and is usually sold in cans. Moreover, in recent years its alcohol content has been cut to a modest 2.8 per cent, to fit in with new British government tax rules that halved the amount of duty paid on beers of this strength.

Being in a can encourages people to keep the beer in a fridge, no bad thing as it is a drink that is a real refresher when chilled. The beer has a deep black colour, with a fine tan head. Its aroma has hints of chocolate and roasted barley; the flavours are relatively mild and easy going. There is some chocolate and some sweetness, but nothing cloying. It might be hard to find on sale, but it is not hard to drink and is worth the effort. And you do not have to be old, an invalid or a nursing mother to enjoy it.

39. PUNK IPA
Style: American IPA
Strength: 5.6% ABV
Brewer: BrewDog
Country of origin: UK
First brewed: 2007

When it comes to brewing and marketing beer, you should 'break all the rules', says BrewDog co-founder James Watt. In his book *Business for Punks*, Watt says in the 1970s punk rock changed the world. 'It was more than just music, it was a cultural phenomenon.' He says the business, which was co-founded with friend Martin Dickie, is built on the punk mentality, which is all about learning the skills to do things on your own terms. The pair were inspired to follow their dreams and set up a brewery after a chance meeting with the late beer writer Michael Jackson. And they certainly took on the conservatism and status quo of the British brewing industry when they set up the company in 2007. They were passionate, didn't give a damn and were irreverently anti-authority. Through their in-your-face marketing and advertising, they were on a mission to offer a rebellion against mass-market beers and bland brands. In their own words, they were anarchic, reckless and tore up the business rule book.

The company imaginatively used crowd-sourcing to raise money and now has a community of thousands of 'equity punk investors' who wanted to share in the craft beer revolution. Well, it remains to be seen how a company could within a few short years have sourced millions of pounds of

investment and be operating bars and breweries on both sides of the Atlantic by breaking all the rules. That is a story for another time.

However, what they did do was fill a vacuum in the beer market – a new generation of drinkers liked what they saw and heard that beer wasn't just for older folks; it suddenly became relevant to the 'now generation'. Beer was as hip as surfing, snowboarding, Hackney-hipster beards and tattoos. And in a very post-punk use of the media, negatives were always turned into positives.

BrewDog hit back at the Portman Group after the alcohol industry watchdog ruled one of its drinks should be removed from shelves for glamorising drugs. The watchdog upheld a complaint about BrewDog's seasonal ale Speedball, which shares a name with the cocktail of crack cocaine and heroin that killed Hollywood stars John Belushi and River Phoenix. Dickie came out fighting, declaring the beer – which has only sold in small quantities in the UK – was named in response to the Portman Group previously targeting its best-selling brews Riptide, Punk IPA and Hop Rocker. He said: 'In the last eight months they were trying to block the sale of our three top-selling beers so this time we thought we would give them something worth banning us for and we accept the name is slightly provocative. The long term view was that we were going to change the name to Dogma anyway.' If there was a headline to be grabbed, they grabbed it.

They set about brewing the world's strongest beer, and gave the world, after a trip to a local ice-cream maker who helped with some cold distillation, Tactical Nuclear Penguin (32 per cent ABV) and Sink the Bismarck (41 per cent ABV). But if that was not enough, then came The End Of History (55 per cent ABV). And to market the beers they even bottled twelve bottles of The End Of History inside seven dead stoats, four squirrels and one hare. And the fans of BrewDog loved the approach. The media lapped it up. The more they did, the bigger their story became.

But rhetoric and swagger will only get people so far. Anyone can sell a bad beer once, selling it twice is near impossible. They had seen how the craft beer movement in America was changing an industry and they wanted to add this rock 'n' roll style to what they did. And as importantly, they wanted to brew great, distinctive beers. Love them, hate them, but you cannot ignore them.

Drawing inspiration for Punk IPA from the bold brashness of some US craft brewers, they created a hop forward beer with exquisite complexity, laden with palate-challenging character. Hops and more hops are added in the brew house and it exudes layers of piney blackcurrant and even passionfruit aromas from the power of its trio of new-wave US aroma hops, Chinook, Crystal and Moteka. Underpinning the hops is a grist made with Maris Otter malt – it might be a 50-year-old variety that is today shunned by many brewers, but the extra pale grain gives a sweet balance to the beer.

True to their word, they took a classic mainstream beer and gave it a contemporary spin with the signature BrewDog bite. So strip away the marketing hype and there is passion and the ability to create and brew some great beers. If they keep going like this, punk will become mainstream.

38. FULLER'S VINTAGE
Style: Barley wine
Strength: 8.5% ABV
Brewer: Fuller's
Country of origin: UK
First brewed: 1997

What started as a simple idea has become a beer with ever-changing layers of liquid complexity.

There always has been a close affinity between brewers either side of the Atlantic. Indeed, since the *Mayflower* first landed in America, brewers have swapped ideas and raw materials. Arguably, one of the most influential beers to cross the Atlantic from East to West was Fuller's Extra Special Bitter (ESB). First brewed in 1969 as a seasonal beer, when it was called Winter Beer, it was renamed ESB and went on in 1971 to be proclaimed as the Campaign for Real Ales' champion beer of Britain. Exported to the USA, it acquired a cult status among beer fans, who marvelled at its complexity, created by pale ale and crystal malts and an aromatic blend of Challenger, Northdown, Target and Golding hops.

America's new wave of craft brewers began to see if they could replicate the beer, which was completely different to 99 per cent of the beers brewed in the USA. And as imitation has to be the sincerest form of flattery, ESB has come to denote a class of beers that are strong in alcohol and rich in aromatic but not assertive hops.

The West London company has a deserved reputation for brewing strong ales. To celebrate Fuller's 150th anniversary in 1995, the then head brewer Reg Drury created 1845. The beer even has a connection to the British royal family: the Prince of Wales threw a handful of hops into the copper as his contribution to the celebrations. A bottle-conditioned beer, Drury was intrigued how over time the beer matured and evolved in the bottle. He was inspired to begin some experiments with how beer changed over time.

So in 1997 the first Vintage Ale was created. The idea was that the beer should be an annual one-off, brewed with different malts and hops but always to the same strength, 8.5 per cent ABV. It is a practice that has continued to this day. It is a beer that takes time and care to make and needs at least five months to brew. It is only produced in relatively limited quantities, between 100 and 200 barrels a year, and so bottles, especially early editions, are much sought after. The beer has gone on to acquire cult status. It's an ale that is much bigger than the sum of its parts.

Chef Sriram Aylur of the Michelin 1-starred restaurant Quilon is a fan of beer. In fact, he is more than a fan of beer, he is a passionate believer that in Britain we should treat our national drink with far greater reverence. He decided his restaurant should not only have a fine wine list, but a beer list too. Based in London's Victoria, around the corner from Buckingham Palace, Quilon is already acclaimed internationally for its five- and eight-course beer menus paired with its south-west coast Indian dishes, and for its international beer list. Aylur introduced the UK's first Vintage Beer List, taking the concept of beer and haute cuisine to a new level. The first Vintage Beer List he put together included eight different vintages of Vintage Ale: 1999, 2002, 2004, 2005, 2006, 2008, 2009 and 2010. Aylur hopes more British brewers will see the gastronomic potential of laying down vintage beers. He said: 'They are

© Fuller's

being sipped not just as digestifs, but as aperitifs as well – and they are appealing particularly well to visiting brewers and to our international customers from India, Europe and Scandinavia. Many female customers are sharing a bottle in preference to stronger brandies and ports.'

The 2008 vintage recently tried had discernible orange notes from the Northdown and Challenger, the alcohol is long and warming. In many beers hops are an uninspired but necessary component, offering little more than an understated bitterness and essential defences against bugs that could turn the beer sour. Not so with this beer, where the hops stand front of stage enjoying the limelight alongside the malted barley.

The 16th Vintage Ale, issued in 2012, used organic barley grown on Sir James Fuller's Neston Park Estate in Wiltshire, which had been specially floor malted by Warminster Malt for Fuller's. The English hops used for both brewing and dry hopping included Golding, Target and Organic Sovereign, from Fuller's Hereford organic hop grower John Walker. A tasting revealed an initial aroma of ripe autumnal fruits with slight notes of rosehips, leading on to a smooth middle palate with just a hint of spice. There is a pleasant hop bitterness, which is then finished with a satisfying orange peel flavour and alcohol warming on the aftertaste.

In its 19th year, the 2015 vintage marked the 50th anniversary of famous British malt variety Maris Otter together with Target, Northdown, Challenger and Golding hops.

Fuller's current head brewer John Keeling said he is proud to be continuing the tradition of brewing Vintage Ale and said: 'Vintage Ale is a truly distinguished bottle-conditioned ale. Each Vintage is a blend of that year's finest malt and hops, and of course our unique yeast, which creates a special limited-edition brew that will only get better with time. I suggest buying a few and trying one now, trying one in five years and trying one in ten years, to see how the flavours have developed and matured.' He says there is no right time to drink a Vintage, saying beer doesn't mature in a linear way, but more like a sine curve.

Labelling legislation means that Fuller's has to put a 'best before' date on the beer. The 2015 vintage's best before date is 2018. As Keeling said: 'Although we are obliged to state a best before date, like a fine wine or whisky, this mellow, bottle-conditioned ale will improve with age for many more years.'

37. JAIPUR
Style: India pale ale
Strength: 5.9% ABV
Brewer: Thornbridge
Country of origin: UK
First brewed: 2005

Some strong beers are too easy to drink.

A friendship forged out of a fierce football rivalry led to the setting up of the Thornbridge brewery in a ten-barrel brewery, housed in the grounds of Thornbridge Hall, near Bakewell, Derbyshire. Jim Harrison, owner of Thornbridge Hall, is an ardent Sheffield Wednesday fan, but his love of real ale took him to the Fat Cat pub owned by the lifelong Sheffield United fan Dave Wickett. He had heard of Wickett's reputation for selling and brewing good beer, because he also owned the adjacent Kelham Island Brewery. And it is quite a reputation: within 15 short years of establishing Kelham

Island, the former lecturer garnered a sackful of awards for the quality and innovation of his brews – including the coveted Campaign for Real Ale Champion Beer of Britain Award in 2004 for Pale Rider.

As director of Sheffield Wednesday's supporters club the Owls Trust, Harrison was always looking for ways to raise funds for the club. And he had seen the success of Wickett's brewing enterprise and his ability to produce special brews to celebrate events in the city of Sheffield as something he could take advantage of. For Harrison wanted the blue and whites to have their own beer, which could be bought by the Wednesday fans to raise money for the club.

And so Hirsty's No. 9, named after David Hirst, one of the team's greats who pulled on the Wednesday shirt for eleven seasons but who through injury never achieved his potential, kicked off the business relationship. 'We first launched a beer with the Trust a few years ago with Hirsty's No. 9, which sold incredibly well', said Harrison.

Well Wickett wouldn't have his beloved blades outdone by a Wednesdayite. So to counter the Wednesday beer he launched Currie's No. 10, celebrating the cavalier life of one of United's finest.

A business relationship was beginning to develop.

At the time Jim Harrison and his wife Emma had just bought Thornbridge Hall, set in 100 acres of stunning parkland, in the heart of the Peak District National Park. Harrison decided he was going to have a brewery in an old, unused stonemason's and joiner's workshop.

Though the friendship persisted, the pair decided not to continue the business relationship, but not before Harrison had helped recruit a studious Italian brewer called Stefano Cossi. Cossi drew on historical sources for some of his beers, such as the full-bodied St Petersburg Stout. But for others, fruits and herbs foraged from Thornbridge's grounds went into the beers. One beer, Bracia, uses an Italian honey, made by bees that had feasted on chestnut blossom.

However, in that frantic first year of creativity it was Jaipur that is likely to be best remembered. The beer is a marvellously hoppy version of an IPA, which draws inspiration from the USA and Burton on Trent. The American influence brings the hops. Lots of fruity and aromatic American hops, Ahtanum, Centennial and Chinook. From England comes Maris Otter pale ale malt, which makes the rich, sweet wort. The beer's name is also a homage to IPA's relationship with India: Thornbridge's version is named after the Indian city of Jaipur, which is famed for its pink buildings.

The beer has massive citrus hop flavours, which are smoothed and rounded by a honey sweetness. It's a beer that starts slowly, but on swallowing the full intensity of complexity is realised as the warmth of the alcohol starts to work.

Time hasn't stood still and in 2010 Thornbridge opened the state of the art Riverside Brewery in nearby Bakewell and while beer volumes have increased, the brewers are still looking for old recipes to which they can add a modern twist in the original brewery. The formula has worked well: it has won more than 250 awards, national and international, since it began.

Currently, at the Hall, several beers are gently ageing in flavoursome wooden barrels that were once used to store spirits. As the beers grow older, intensity, acidity and spirit notes will be added to their taste.

To mark the 10th anniversary of Jaipur's creation, Thornbridge's new head brewer Rob Lovatt produced an imperial version of the beer, Jaipur X. At 10 per cent ABV, it's strong and hop forward. The aroma is grapefruit, mango

and marmalade orange with a lingering, if sticky, bitter finish. And like its illustrious junior, it is too easy to drink.

36. BROADSIDE
Style: Strong bitter
Strength: 6.3% and 4.7% ABV
Brewer: Adnams
Country of origin: UK
First brewed: 1972

The cannons flared. The cannons roared. And so on the morning of 6 June 1672, the Battle of Sole Bay began.

Most people don't know that there was one Anglo-Dutch War, let alone a second, but this was the first naval exchange of the third. A fleet of 75 ships from the Dutch Republic surprised a joint Anglo-French fleet of 93 ships at anchor in Sole Bay, near Southwold in Suffolk. And after a bloody day of battle, which saw many die, the sound of the guns ceased with both sides claiming victory. Possibly it was only the townsfolk of Southwold who did well out of the battle because the town's records show anyone who found the body of a drowned sailor was paid a shilling (5p) to bury it. And because at least 3,800 died on that fateful day, there was some money to be made. Today Southwold is better known as the home of the Adnams Brewery.

A pier, a lighthouse, beach huts and some fabulously intimate pubs all make the town of Southwold on England's east coast stand out from the crowd. However, in the shadow of the lighthouse, it is the brewery where in 1345 the 'alewives' of the town made beer that makes it truly memorable. In 1872, two brothers, George (who was later eaten by a crocodile in Africa) and Ernest Adnams, bought the brewery with an inheritance from their father. The 140-year-old brewery now has the reputation for making some quintessentially English ales and for being the 'greenest' brewery in Europe.

The production of its 'beers from the coast' is overseen by Fergus Fitzgerald. As the head brewer he has to turn his hand to many things, including the introduction of eco-friendly technology. However, his passion is not just the brewing of traditional ale, he is revelling in exploring the limits to which styles can be pushed – be it low strength or higher alcohol beers – cask or keg. American hops, champagne yeast and spices can all be found in the brew house, but it is a traditional strong English bitter that is probably the company's best-known beer.

When it comes to naming beers, it is not unusual for British brewers to seek out military connections when looking for a name for a new beer. Spitfire, Lancaster Bomber, Flagship, Bombadier and Victory Ale are names often seen on pump clips in pubs. So when Adnams was looking for a name to commemorate the 300th anniversary of the battle that no one really won, and certainly didn't see Britannia, let alone the Dutch, ruling the seas, they chose Broadside. When it was first brewed, it was a bottled beer only, at a robust 6.3 per cent ABV. It was a beer to be sipped and savoured. Have too many and you'd be slipped and slavered. However, in 1988 the decision was taken to produce a cask version, but at a lower strength, so great care was taken to see if a 4.7 per cent draught version could be produced that had similar characteristics. Well, they do have similar tastes, both malty and fruitcake flavours, but the bottled Broadside certainly has a bigger bang.

© Adnams

Brewed with pale ale, chocolate malt and First Gold hops, Broadside is a dark, ruby red beer rich in fruitcake aromas, almonds and conserved fruit. It is a multi-award winner, including Best Strong Bitter in the country, and was awarded a gold medal at the Great British Beer Festival.

The British have been using the word bitter since the early 19th century, though it was more than 100 years before the term became widely used. The style, such as it is, covers a wide range of colours, flavours and strengths. The term bitter probably came into common use before the use of pump clips to identify different beers or brands. Brewers probably called their beer a pale ale, but drinkers started to identify them as bitter. Because there was nothing on the bar to identify the beer as a pale ale, they would ask for a bitter, to show they didn't want the sweeter less-hopped mild.

Drinking a pint of Broadside in a pub on Sole Bay is a sheer joy. The mouthfeel is full and the taste is dominated by blackberries and other dark fruit that vie for attention with the rich, roasted sweet, caramel malt. It's rich but not overwhelming. There are lots of hops and spice on the nose. This is affordable luxury at its best.

35. TARAS BOULBA
Style: Belgian ale
Strength: 4.5% ABV
Brewer: De la Senne
Country of origin: Belgium
First brewed: 2006

Always remember, an easy-drinking beer can have layers and layers of complexity.

Bernard Leboucq and Yvan De Baets are two of Belgium's most talented new wave of brewers. They say they are resolute in their desire to create beers that are big in flavour, but low in alcohol. And they want to make beers they would like to drink themselves. They are also determined to see Brussels be once again a place renowned for brewing excellence and to ensure that the country's lost beer styles are not forgotten. And to this end they spend much time researching original sources for long-lost recipes.

The pair opened De la Senne in December 2010, though they had been brewing together since 2003 when they set up their first brewery in the small town of Sint-Pieters-Leeuw. However, they soon outgrew the space. And like many other young, ambitious beer creators, they became known as gypsy brewers. This meant renting space in other people's breweries, usually their friends', where they could create their own beers.

But the lure of their own brewery in their home city was too much. And with the opening of De la Senne, for the first time in many years, there was another brewery in addition to Cantillon in the city. Friends but not rivals. The brewery's

© De la Senne

name pays homage to the Senne Valley and its river, which is so important to the region's brewing story. For it is here, drifting in the air, hiding in cobwebs and lurking in cracks in old wooden beams, that can be found the curious wild yeasts so vital for making the region's palate-challenging lambic beers.

Belgium has a chequered history, with France, Germany, Britain and the Netherlands all influencing the country's proud brewing heritage. It has seen more ancient brewing traditions continue through to the current day than any other country. It is for this reason the country's brewing has been so influential on the craft beer movement all around the world.

Belgium is also renowned for its weird and wild comics and animation. It is with good reason that Belgian cartoonists and animators are regarded as some of the best in the world. Great artwork can be found on many of the labels of beers brewed in Flanders. Some of the most distinctive are the entrancing mix of modern and vintage propaganda images used by De la Senne.

The label on Taras Boulba depicts a corruption of a story written by the Russian author Gogol and seems to involve an angry father berating a man, possibly his son, for marrying someone outside his religion, politics and language. The label says that this is only the beginning of the story. Well, we shall see. The story the beer tells in the glass is one of brewing excellence. Taras Boulba is a light blonde ale, which looks hazy gold in the glass. It bubbles with a citrus hop bitterness. The nose is of fresh bread, some spice, fresh spring flowers and seductive teasing of the pleasures to come.

The Belgian ale yeast exudes some spicy flavours, even a hint of lemongrass, and brings a pleasing fruitiness balanced by the crispness of the pilsner malt and wheat. It is much lighter in colour than a typical English pale ale. De Baets says Taras Boulba is a session beer, which pairs well with many food dishes, particularly creamy cheese. This makes it a favourite with people at lunchtime or those popping into a bar on their way home after a day at work.

Most De La Senne beers are under 5 per cent ABV, but there are a couple of stronger beers in its portfolio, which De Baets says should be reserved for special occasions. De La Senne's Zwarte Piet, at 8 per cent ABV, is a strong dark ale with aromas of dark chocolate, dried plums, prunes, figs and vanilla. It is a beer to be relished, slowly sipped and enjoyed with dark unsweetened chocolate or even a hard, well-matured Belgian cheese.

But for easy drinking, try the Taras Boulba.

34. PETRUS OUD BRUIN

Style: Flemish brown ale
Strength: 5.5% ABV
Brewer: De Brabandere
Country of origin: Belgium
First brewed: 1970s

One of the greatest sights in the beer world has to be the large storage room in the Brabandere brewery in Bavikhove, in the heart of one of Belgium's best-known brewing regions, Flanders. Here stand the large 220 hectolitre French oak foeders, which quietly go about their business of ageing and souring beer. The large wooden storage vessels are often known as tuns, and it is in these that the aged, pale beer used in the blend for Petrus Oud Bruin slowly matures.

© De Brabandere

The family-owned brewery, whose surname gives the brewery its name, was founded in 1894. Like many Belgian brewing families, the Brabanderes began as farmers and used their own grains to make beer. Its beer Petrus Oud Bruin is a classic blend of one-third Petrus Aged Pale, pure foeder beer and two-thirds young brown beer. This beer is liquid heritage and the brewery is rightly proud of its motto 'never compromise on taste'.

Possibly all beers were once made in this way and it's a tradition the brewery is proud to have revitalised, the blending of beers old and new. Both Belgium and the UK have a tradition of making beers in this way. The ageing of beer in wood allows a lactic fermentation to take place and some additional conditioning from the slow-working brewing yeasts, which often reveals characteristics not present when the beer first ferments.

The ageing turns the beer slightly sour, similar to an oak-aged wine. And similar to a wine that needs blending to bring out its true character, the flavour spikes will be softened by the addition of a younger beer. The addition of the young, dark beer not only softens the beer's sourness but gives it its characteristic reddish brown colour. Even though the aged beer is in the barrel for 24 months, the brewer doesn't want the beer to taste of oak. Instead, the foeder provides a fertile breeding ground for various microorganisms that convert the remaining sugars in the beer from the prime fermentation into acids, higher alcohols and esters. The wood is also semi-permeable and allows air to come in contact with the beer. Over the two years the beer slowly oxidises, and becomes a refreshing, palate-cleansing fruity, sour, aromatic beer.

The sweet and sour style was once very common across Flanders – in the east of the region it is often called brown or bruin, head west and it usually becomes known as red. But Petrus Oud Bruin is an exception to this rule.

A blended old ale with a long heritage can be found in England: Strong Suffolk, which is made by Greene King. Moreover, many of the country's new wave of brewers are rediscovering the art of storing beer in wood and then blending it. One such is Burning Sky, where the brewers are experimenting with making a Sussex version of a Flanders beer. The aim is a deeper, more complex taste. The brewer must be careful, though, because excess wood tannins can also be introduced to the beer, affecting it in a negative way. Barrel ageing is especially suitable for the amber brown beers of Flanders, which rely on grain and malt for flavour and not aromatic hops.

Petrus Oud Bruin has a deep, almost a rusted, Burgundy colour. The taste is light and refreshing. Wheat and a blend of pale ale and crystal malts are used in the grist; that cocktail of grains adds to the beer's refreshing qualities. Ruby red to the eye, it is easy to see why it is known as the Burgundy of Flanders. Its aroma swirls with red fruit flavours. It is a complex harmony of sweet and sour, which feels sensuous on the tongue. There are flavours of plum, prune, raisin and black cherry. Who needs a glass of red wine when one can drink a beer like this?

33. GRAND CRU
Style: Belgian red ale
Strength: 6% ABV
Brewer: Rodenbach
Country of origin: Belgium
First brewed: 1895

There is something remarkably independent about the people of Flanders. And that streak of self-determination is exemplified by the number of breweries that brew world-class, distinctive beers. Rodenbach brewery is located in the town of Roeselare in West Flanders, north-west Belgium, which is famed for its sour red ales.

Pedro Rodenbach, whose family originally came from the German Rhineland, became a partner in the Roeselare brewery in 1821, and bought it outright in 1836. However, it was his grandson Eugène who developed the beer that the brewery has become famous for. Eugène travelled to England in the 1870s. Here he studied the art and craft of making porter – learning about ageing beer in wood, the development of lactic flavours and blending. And it was these new skills that he brought back to the brewery.

Today, beneath the brewing hall at the brewery is a large cellar that is home to 300 foeders. These oak vats, or tuns, vary in size from 140 hectolitres up to a massive 650 hectolitres. It is here, in these vessels that embrace the beer for up to two years, that the sweet and sour magic of Grand Cru is created. It is with good reason that the brewer employs its own coopers to maintain the vessels, one of which dates back to 1868 and many to the 1900s.

Rodenbach beers are brewed with a blend of pale ale and coloured malts, especially Vienna Red. Some hops from Poperinge are used, but they are likely to be a couple of years old. The brewer wants them not for their aromatic qualities, which are present in fresh hops, but just for their ability to act as a preservative.

The beer is fermented in large, tall steel vessels with a multi-strain yeast (according to scientists at the University of Leuven it contains more than twenty different cultures), before being put into horizontal tanks for lagering for one month. This starts the process of producing the lactic flavours, anaerobically. Then, and only then, it is transferred into one of the wooden tuns. Here the beer is left to age for 24 months or so, where the many bacteria in the wood create a complex tapestry of sour fruit flavours. The porosity of the wood means the beer comes in contact with air and the lactic fermentation continues to weave its magic.

Rodenbach's regular sour beer, the Classic, is usually blended with a young un-soured beer and an aged beer in the ratio of three to one. However, the soaring Grand Cru is two-thirds aged beer with one-third young beer, which is added to temper the assertive sour flavours. And the final touch is the addition of a little sugar. 'It's the best of two worlds', said Rodenbach's master brewer Rudi Ghequire. 'You add a young beer to tone down the sourness of the beer.'

The Grand Cru is a world classic, and so it is hardly surprising that it has won many golds in competitions around the world. A ruby brown colour, it has aromas of fruit and a hint of turmeric and a soft chord of balsamic vinegar. There is Madeira sherry and passionfruit. Its taste is sweet and sour, with a hint of umami. There are red fruits and wonderful swirls of lactic, and it finishes long and dry, similar to a quinine-flavoured aperitif.

© Rodenbach

The beer pairs sublimely with food – olives, pickled vegetables and fish can all duet harmoniously with its assertive character. But it also works with game and liver. This is a beer not just for any occasion, but also special occasions.

Once an advertisement for Rodenbach described the beer as wine. Well, the beer does have some of the exquisite tannins that one would expect to find in a great grand cru Burgundian wine. But no wine, not even the greatest in the world, could ever be as thirst-quenching or refreshing. Beer is clearly the best long drink in the world.

32. SAISON DUPONT

Style: Saison
Strength: 6.5% ABV
Brewer: Brasserie Dupont
Country of origin: Belgium
First brewed: 1930s

There was a time when most farmhouses in northern Europe made their own beers. It is likely that most were seasonal brews – brewed in the cooler months of winter and intended for consumption over a hot summer when brewing, because of the heat, was much harder to do.

Yeast, that essential component for turning sugar into alcohol as part of its lifecycle, doesn't thrive if the ambient temperature is too high. In addition, the warmer temperatures are more likely to create conditions in which bacteria can prosper and spoil the beer. Perhaps this is why some of the best saisons often have a swirl and caress of lactic acid. The original saisons were made in an era before refrigeration, and often spices and other botanicals would be added to disguise any spoilage in the beer. The bonus of a spicy addition is that, like the botanicals in a good gin, they make it easy drinking and super refreshing.

Most of these seasonal farmhouse brews have long since disappeared, though many of the new-wave craft US brewers are producing their variant of the style. However, in the Hainault region of Wallonia, which is close to the French border, the practice of brewing a seasonal beer has continued. But once where there were hundreds of breweries, there are now just a few. Widely known as saisons, which means season in French, examples of these beers can still be found. A malty variant of the style is also brewed just over the border in France, which is known as Bière de Garde.

Brasserie Dupont is located in Tourpes, in the centre of West Hainault. Despite being a modern brewery, it is still part of a farm that dates back to 1759. According to some records, brewing has been going on here since 1844, but no one would be surprised if it had started earlier. The brewery still uses its aged coal-fired kettle. It is said the intensity of the flame under the copper depends on how strong the wind is that day and the direction it comes from.

It is hard to define what makes a Saison. Originally, they were made by farmers who probably just used what was to hand. Top-fermenting beers, these were beers for personal consumption and not commercial products. Recipes, if they existed, were probably not written down. They could be light or dark, hoppy or spicy, sweet or dry. However, Dupont is regarded as producing the definitive and probably best example of the style. Though it has to be said, its current strength of 6.5 per cent ABV does seem a little strong for a lunchtime drink. Earlier variants were probably around 4.5 per cent.

© Brasserie Dupont

But the variation is the beguiling attraction of the style. Originally the beers would have varied from beers low in alcohol, which children could safely drink (the health and energy drinks of the day), to table strength beer and families would sit around their table eating hunks of bread, goat's cheese and cured meats while quenching their thirst.

Unfiltered in the bottle, the beer is a hazy yellow and beautifully balanced. And drinkers shouldn't be concerned if there is some sediment in the bottle or poured into the glass. This is a living beer which is bottled with yeast, *sur lies*. Ageing wine on the lees is common practice for white Burgundy and other Chardonnay-style wines, but it is also a technique used by brewers.

The beer is hopped with Kent Golding, which gives a gentle hint of orange fruit and a touch of spice. The finish is long and dry, leaving the drinker ready for another sip. The beer is soft on the tongue and even has some cheesy aromas. Add to this some tart and citrus zesty notes and the result is a beer that is very refreshing. It is a perfect partner to many foods, especially spicy sausages and a venison or beer stew flavoured with juniper.

Today, Dupont's beers are known well beyond its farmhouse roots. Its future was probably saved by the decision to export beers in 1992. They now produce more than 2 million hectolitres of beer, 40 per cent of which is destined for export to countries such as the USA, Japan, Canada, Italy, the Netherlands, France, Denmark and Great Britain. However, success has not dimmed the ambition of the owners to stick to their artisanal, farmhouse roots.

31. FRIDAY'S PALE ALE
Style: American pale ale
Strength: 4.7% ABV
Brewer: Septem
Country of origin: Greece
First brewed: 2009

A Greek beer is one of the best in the world? Surely not. Most people's experience of a Greek beer is a refreshing lager-style beer, probably drunk after a day on a sun-kissed beach. Thirst quenching yes, but world class?

Well things have changed. The country has experienced its own beer revolution in the last few years and today there are more than 30 small brewers. It has not yet caught up with the innovative and creative brewing taking place in Italy or Spain. But the country that celebrates Dionysus the god of wine now rejoices in the grain and hop too. For Septem's Pale Ale is no Greek myth, it's the real thing.

Situated on the large Greek island of Evia near Athens, the second largest after Crete and linked to the mainland by an attractive and much used new bridge, Septem Microbrewery was set up by chemist and oenologist Sophocles Panagiotou and economist Georgios Panagiotou. Sophocles wanted to bring his wine-making skills to beer and show that different hop varieties were as important to beer as grapes are to wine. He brings with him the skill of blending and understanding the influence of wood barrels on wine and a future project involves putting beer into oak barrels. Clearly it was a bold move to set aside the grape and replace it with malt and hops and establish a craft brewery that could as easily grace California as a Greek island.

Sophocles has bold ambitions for the brewery, as he is also planting his own small hop garden, about 2.5 hectares in size. The island's Mediterranean climate makes it difficult for English hops to thrive, but he is hoping the American variety Cascade will prosper. His focus is on fresh, unpasteurised beer with a wealth of aromas and flavours. In Latin the name Septem means seven, which represents the number of days, plus one day of rest, it took to make the Earth. The brewery makes one beer for each day of the week, and Fridays is its Pale Ale. However, unsurprisingly the Septem week is already more than seven days – there is an eighth day and several specials including a green-hopped beer.

And as in the children's nursery rhyme that describes Friday's child as loving and giving, this beer is one that deserves to be given time and consideration. It is in no way surprising that Septem was recently named the best brewer in Europe by the acclaimed International Beer Challenge competition.

Septem's Pale Ale is an American pale ale (APA), a style of pale ale developed in the United States around 1980. Derived from a British beer, typically American pale ales are around 5 per cent ABV, with significant quantities of American hops, typically Cascade. The beer should have fruity hop and citrus aromas, perhaps some grassy notes with only a restrained hint of malt or caramel. However, Sophocles has given his APA a Bohemian and New Zealand hop twist, which is cleverly and subtly underpinned by English Maris Otter pale ale malt. The malted grain of choice for many of the world's greatest real ale brewers.

The noble hop Saaz, originally from the town of Saaz in Bohemia in what is now the Czech Republic, brings a soft, herbal character to the beer. However, it is the New Zealand hop Nelson Sauvin that brings swathes of white grape and tropical flavours of mango, pineapple and passionfruit to the beer.

The beer fills the glass with shards of golden Greek sunshine. The aroma has exotic tropical notes and indeed it could be glass of a great white wine. The malt is subdued but provides a diligent foundation to a great beer. Friday's beer is full of grace and dignity, and unsurprisingly it works well with food, particularly fish. What could be better than sitting in a café on the edge of the Adriatic, watching the waves caress the sand and sipping a glass of Septem's Pale Ale together with a plate of fish freshly caught that day? Some beer moments are near perfect. This beer isn't just for Friday, it is for every day – and it is not just first class, but world class.

Beware the Greeks? Never, instead celebrate the country's new wave of craft brewers.

30. KÖLSCH
Style: Kölsch
Strength: 4.8% ABV
Brewer: Früh
Country of origin: Germany
First brewed: 1948

It looks like a glass of classic golden pilsner, but it's not. This is no cold-fermented lager beer stored in a deep cave for many weeks at zero degrees. Instead, it's a light, almost straw-coloured, golden ale that can officially only be brewed in the Cologne area of Germany. It is truly a special beer, made with

top- or warm-fermented yeast, even though it is fermented at lower temperatures than are traditionally associated with an ale. It is always best drunk fresh on draught, and preferably within the shadow of Cologne's historic cathedral.

The beer is a survivor of a time when the great brewing nation of Germany was home to all sorts of unusual beers, many of which would qualify as ales and not the lagers for which the country is rightly renowned.

The term Kölsch seems to have started to come into common use around 1918, when it was attributed to a beer from the Sünner brewery. It was a filtered version of an earlier cloudier style and its golden sheen made it popular with people who preferred their beer clear. And soon the term Kölsch became the generic term for any golden ale brewed in the city. In 1948 the brewers of Cologne came together to agree guidelines for the beer. In truth the guidelines are a little vague, but the beer should be top fermented, golden and have a good hop character.

Today, it is a beer with its own geographic appellation. Since 1985, no brewer outside the city of Cologne or some nearby villages can call its beer a Kölsch. However, other brewers do try and get around the rule by stating they brew a 'kölsch-style' beer.

Früh is regarded as one of the best examples of the style and the most famous place to drink it is the brewery's tap, close to the cathedral. The tap is where Peter Josef Früh established his brewery in 1904, in a building that was formerly a theatre. The building was destroyed in 1944, but thankfully the family had another brewery not far away, where the beer is still brewed today.

Kölsch is a light and subtle beer that reveals itself slowly. There are delicate flavours of malt and fruit, followed by a soft sweetness. It's an easy-drinking beer. Served fresh, it should be full of light malt and floral fruit flavours; apple or pear characteristics might even be detected. The beer has much in common with alt, the local beer from the nearby Rhineland city of Düsseldorf.

Traditionally it is served by self-employed waiters known as kobes. They usually wear long aprons and carry a leather money purse. If served properly, the beer arrives in a small, cylindrical glass called a stange from a round tray designed to carry many glasses of the beer without spilling any. It is an elegant glass, which only holds 200 ml of beer. We drink as much with our eyes as our taste buds and the glass's proportions perfectly display the golden body and white foam head of the beer. The waiters will keep bringing fresh glasses of the beer until the drinker places a beer mat on top of an empty glass, signifying no more beer is needed and that you are ready to pay your bill.

It is a beer that would be overwhelmed by strong flavours of some foods, but a simple plate of cheese and sausage is an ideal companion.

29. VELVET MERKIN
Style: Oatmeal stout
Strength: 8.5% ABV
Brewer: Firestone Walker
Country of origin: USA
First brewed: 2004

There was a time when many British brewers made an oatmeal stout. It could have well been in response to a demand for beers to be more nutritious. However, by the 1950s the fashion had all but died out in the UK. Perhaps it was because oats are not an easy grain to put into a mash tun. Too much can quickly create a sticky, gloopy porridge, which jams valves and pipes.

However, we probably have brewers in the USA to thank for keeping the style going and for developing it to new heights. Back in the 1970s and 80s, the then new wave of US brewers turned to Europe and history books for beers to brew and discovered oatmeal stouts. Then a US importer commissioned an oatmeal stout from the Samuel Smith brewery in Tadcaster, Yorkshire, and several brewers tried to make their own version. Today, probably hundreds are being made.

The founders of the brewery, David Walker and Adam Firestone, are fascinated by the influence that wood has on the taste of beer. Early experiments using former Chardonnay casks were not particularly successful. The barrels were infected and the beer produced couldn't even be used as vinegar. However, they were determined to persist with their experiments. Their brewmaster Matt Brynildson went on to develop the company's system for fermenting beers in wood, inspired by the Burton Union system, which was developed in England in the 1840s, where a series of linked wooden barrels collects the excess yeast and foam created during the brewing process.

However, the Firestone variant is much more than a yeast collector. The oak barrels add taste to the beer. A batch of beer will begin its fermentation in a steel vessel and then a portion is put into the wooden barrels for about a week, before it is blended back in again. According to Brynildson, it creates a depth of flavour unattainable when using a beer solely fermented in a steel vessel.

© Firestone Walker

Velvet Merkin started life as a shy and retiring beer at 5.5 per cent ABV. It was first brewed when Brynildson was a home brewer. However, for the first commercial brews the beer's name was changed to Velvet Merlin. At the time it was thought that the world was not ready for a beer that shared its name with a pubic wig.

The beer's mash bill contains seven different grains; 63 per cent is pale malt, 12 per cent roasted barley and 12 per cent oats. This helps create a deep, black beer with a rich texture. US-grown Fuggles hops add some bitterness, but not too much. Brynildson said: 'I can't remember when we first brewed it. My guess would be at least 10 years ago. I can tell you that it was a tasting room-only beer for a while and we called it Velvet Merkin before we called it Merlin. It was a homebrew recipe I brought with me, which I had first brewed in my garage in Kalamazoo, Michigan back in 1994.'

A few years after Velvet Merlin was put on sale, Brynildson began experimenting with putting beers into barrels that had once contained spirits, including the Merlin. It was time for the name Merkin to be unveiled again. The beer is aged for a full year in retired Woodford Reserve bourbon barrels from Heaven Hill. The rich Kentucky bourbon is renowned for its smooth rounded citrus, cinnamon and cocoa flavours, which are overlaid with toffee, caramel, chocolate and spice notes.

Brynildson says the beer ages well in bourbon barrels and delivers rich milk chocolate, bourbon and espresso flavours, preceded by aromas of vanilla, coconut, toasted oak and mocha. It is a big, balanced beer, which despite its size is remarkably restrained. It is only released annually and every vintage will have its own character.

Since it was founded in 1996, the philosophy at Firestone Walker has been to try and brew the perfect beer. I'm not sure if something can be better than perfect, but if it can, then this is that beer.

28. SPARKLING ALE

Style: Australian pale ale
Strength: 5.8% ABV
Brewer: Coopers
Country of origin: Australia
First brewed: 1862

Wherever colonists from northern Europe went, they took brewing technology with them. Across the world there are examples of breweries set up by Dutch and German settlers determined that in their new location they should be able to enjoy a taste of home.

The crew and passengers of the *Mayflower* took brewing equipment to America, and so it was when Australia was colonised. Immigrants to Australia brought big thirsts and by 1890 the country had over 350 breweries. Farmers also reacted quickly to this demand. Hops and barley have been grown in Australia for more than 150 years. But, of those brewers slaking the thirsts of Australians in the 19th century, Coopers is the only survivor of that boom. The beer is living history, a cultured reminder of beer in the 19th century.

It's an ale-style beer, as is Australia's most popular beer, VB. It is only the rest of the world that believes Foster's lager is the country's most popular beer. Indeed, Coopers firmly stuck to its ale roots when many thought it should lagerise its production and give up on bottle-conditioned cloudy ales. For

this is no ice-cold lager sold in a chilled glass, but a bright and breezy link with Australia's proud brewing history. However, the company does produces a highly drinkable lager beer, Crown Gold, for those who prefer their beer well chilled.

A Yorkshire émigré to South Australia, Thomas Cooper, created Coopers Sparkling Ale. It's a light, golden beer with a great white head and a swirling bitterness from the Australian hops and it's a classic. The company is still family owned and is the largest Australian-owned brewery. All the country's other brewers are owned by brewers with head offices in other countries.

Today the beer is made with Pride of Ringwood hops, grown in Tasmania and Victoria, a variety developed in 1959. It is regarded as one of the highest 'alpha' hops in the world, which means its flavour profile is bitter. The hop adds peppery, herbaceous and even woody notes to the beer, but not much in the way of aromatics. The hop's flavour profile differs from those often preferred by the new wave of craft brewers worldwide, who prefer to use aromatic hops. Galaxy, with its floral, citrus, passionfruit notes, is the hop of choice for most of today's new wave of Australian boutique brewers.

The colour is an amber gold, created by the pale, crystal and roasted malts, plus a little sugar. The original beer was an interpretation of the Burton India Pale Ale, so it is pale, strong and entrancingly bitter. It is also bottle conditioned, which means that the beer is living in the bottle, and if it is not poured carefully it will be cloudy in the glass. Pour it quickly and the result is a cloudy haze. Use a steady hand and the beer is bright and amber clear.

The brewery is adamant that while the beer has evolved over time, it is still true to its tradition. The coolships have gone, as have the open wooden fermenting vessels. And the original multi-strain yeast has been cleaned up and is now just a single strain. But the brewers insist the beer is still true to type and the bright amber colour was retained.

And it still stayed a living beer, which means that a little bit of brewing yeast and a touch of sugar are put into every bottle. This makes it beloved by home brewers who wish to try and replicate the beer in their own kitchens. They buy a bottle, carefully pour and drink the beer to avoid it going cloudy and keep the yeasty lees to ferment their own brews.

The company is now experimenting with stronger versions of its ale, which are matured in wood. One such is the Extra Strong Vintage Ale and, just like Coopers Sparkling Ale, the resultant beer is constantly evolving and flying to new heights. It's full of fruit, fruit cake and some citrus on the nose.

Coopers is also encouraging people to try to brew their own version of its Sparkling Ale at home. Inspired by the beer, many home brew enthusiasts will collect the yeast from a bottle they've drunk. However, a lot of care and attention will be needed to brew anything as drinkable as this classic ale.

27. BLACK BUTTE
Style: Porter
Strength: 5.2% ABV
Brewer: Deschutes Brewery
Country of origin: USA
First brewed: 1988

Since the end of Prohibition in 1933, when beer production in the USA legally resumed after a thirteen-year hiatus, most

© Deschutes Brewery

Americans have drunk light-coloured beer. And then along came the craft beer revolution.

Good beer brings people together and that is something Deschutes has been doing since 1988. And the beer that started it all for the brewery, which opened in a public house in Bend, Oregon, was Black Butte Porter. The beer is named after Black Butte, a stratovolcano in Oregon that dominates the skyline, and it is said the beer is the same colour as the jet black lava.

From its modest beginnings, the brewery in the north-west of the country is now one of the biggest craft brewers in the USA. It is planning to open a new brewery in the east of the country in downtown Roanoke, Virginia. The brewery, which was originally founded by restauranteur Gary Fish, has explored hundreds of potential locations in America's east over the last two years before coming to its decision. It wanted to find a location that reflected the same aspirations as in Oregon: a family- and employee-owned brewery that believes in caring for the environment, sustainability and enjoying beer with friends and strangers. 'We started Deschutes Brewery when craft beer wasn't burgeoning and led with a beer style that wasn't popular at the time – Black Butte Porter', said Fish. 'This pioneering approach was a key driver behind our decision to go with Roanoke, as that same spirit exists in this community and its fast-growing beer culture.'

Porter was developed in London, England, and was the first beer to be widely sold commercially in the early 18th century. Developments in malting techniques meant that maltsters were better able to control the roasting of barley to a dark colour without burning it to a cinder. To balance the roast coffee flavour, hops were usually added.

Thanks to the work of brewery historian Martyn Cornell, the origins of porter are now much better understood. One of the biggest myths busted is that the beer was created by a Ralph Harwood in 1772 to replace a style pulled from a trio of beer casks called three threads. It is a nice and oft-repeated story, but porter certainly existed long before this. Another myth is that the beer was named after market porters; it's not far wrong, but instead the beer was named after river and street porters.

It seems likely that porter was in fact London brown beer, a style that was sold as either mild or stale. Porter was a synonym for brown beer and the drink of the working classes. Interestingly the words mild and stale had different definitions in the 1700s. Mild meant fresh beer and stale was more expensive because it had been matured and was at its best. Stale didn't mean, then as it does now, something that is past its best. Confusingly for any beer historian, stout beers weren't necessarily the dark beers we think of today. Stout means strong, so it would have been quite possible to have a pale stout.

Deschutes' variant of porter is a dark beer. It has notes of rich chocolate and coffee, a luscious creaminess and a roasted finish. It has lots of hops (Cascade, Bravo and Tettnang), which give the beer its distinctive aroma.

At the time most Americans drank pale, fizzy yellow beers, so it must have been a brave business move to concentrate on producing a dark beer. It went on to become the first American dark beer to find widespread popularity in the USA and it is now sold worldwide. Black Butte is indeed a black beauty.

26. BOURBON COUNTY
Style: Imperial dry stout
Strength: 14.2% ABV
Brewer: Goose Island
Country of origin: USA
First brewed: 1992

Social media activity erupted in March 2011 when brewing behemoth Anheuser-Busch InBev announced it was to buy Goose Island. Could it be true that the Chicago-based brewpub, which was founded in 1988 when the craft beer industry was still in its infancy in Midwest America, was now supping with the devil?

Goose Island was founded by beer-lover John Hall, who developed Chicago's interest in craft beer by allowing consumers to observe the brewing process – a then novel experience – and enjoy a wide variety of distinctive beers that had been produced on-site. Hall's desire was not just to cater to consumer tastes, but to challenge them. And now he'd sold out?

The blogs were busy and many were tormented by the notion that Goose Island had sold its craft beer soul. Yet the coolest head in town belonged to John Hall himself, who said the move would allow the brewery to expand. And he stressed that the brewery's recipes would be sacrosanct. Hall said: 'Demand for our beers has grown beyond our capacity to serve our wholesale partners, retailers, and beer lovers. This partnership between our extraordinary artisanal brewing team and one of the best brewers in the world in Anheuser-Busch will bring resources to brew more beer here in Chicago to reach more beer drinkers, while continuing our development of new beer styles. This agreement helps us achieve our goals with an ideal partner who helps fuel our growth, appreciates our products and supports their success.'

Greg Hall, son of brewery founder John Hall, has quite a reputation for developing characterful beers and has won plaudits around the world for beers that include Honkers Ale, 312 Urban Wheat Ale and Matilda.

It also broke new ground in 1992 when it wanted to celebrate the 1,000th brew at its original brewpub, but what to do?

By chance, Greg Hall attended a drinks industry dinner and found himself next to Jim Beam's Booker Noe – the man who is credited with breathing new life into the bourbon business. Hall mentioned an idea he had about ageing beer in a bourbon barrel. Before the dinner was complete, a handshake deal had been reached. Greg Hall was breaking new ground.

He put his imperial stout into barrels for 100 days. The beer was as dark and dense as a black hole with thick foam the colour of a bourbon barrel. Its nose was a cocktail of charred oak, chocolate, vanilla, caramel and smoke. It became an instant hit sold on draught in the brewpub and became a bottled beer in 2004. It led to the creation of a whole new category of barrel-aged beers.

Now, each year on Black Friday, the day after Thanksgiving, a new iteration of the beer is released. Fans mark the date in their diaries and queue outside liquor stores waiting to get a bottle of the new release. The success of the beer saw in 2015 six varieties of the beer released, including a barley wine, a coffee stout and a barrel-aged maple syrup as well as the Bourbon County Stout.

The 2015 Bourbon County Stout version of the beer was put in white oak barrels that in 1978 were freshly charred

and filled with Heaven Hill Distilleries' finest whiskey. The whiskey was left to mature for more than 30 years. After bottling, the barrels were acquired by Goose Island and filled with its Imperial Stout and left for a further two years in its Chicago barrel house.

The beer has long notes of tar, tobacco and vanilla. It has a long bittersweet finish and notes of whiskey. According to those who know, it is always best to buy a number of bottles of the beer. One to drink now, another for three months' time and so on, just to see how it changes over time.

It is hardly surprising that people queue for this beer.

25. IMPERIAL STOUT
Style: Imperial stout
Strength: 9% ABV
Brewer: Nøgne Ø
Country of origin: Norway
First brewed: 2005

There are few beers as uncompromising as a full-bodied imperial stout. How appropriate that one of the best in the world comes from the Nøgne Ø brewery on Grimstad's rock-hewn coastline. Here, in winter, the nights and days are dark and the winds are as strong as the brewery's imperial stout Dark Horizon, which is an occasional brew, with a strength often exceeding 16 per cent ABV. However, it is the brewery's Imperial Stout, with a more modest 9 per cent ABV, which stands tall on the world stage. The beer is a clever, three-way bold harmony of sweetness, bitterness

© Nøgne Ø

and darkness. The great depth of flavour and ebony colour come from roasted and dark chocolate malt. It's a swirling duet of rich sweet malt flavours and bitterness from the aromatic hops.

Imperial stouts are among the richest of the beer styles in the world. They are history in a bottle. The style is a development of London porter, but a stronger, fuller bodied version. It garnered its title after being supplied to the imperial court of Czarina Catherine the Great. Back in the 18th century it was the Barclay Perkins Russian Imperial Stout, from London, which was regarded as the definitive example of the style. Probably stronger than 12 per cent ABV, it would have been fulsomely bitter as some 5 kg of hops were put into every barrel.

Nøgne Ø takes its name from a phrase meaning 'naked island', which was used by celebrated playwright Henrik Ibsen in a poem to describe the barren outcrops off Norway's coast. But there is nothing barren about Nøgne Ø's beers. The brewery was founded by Kjetil Jikiun and Gunnar Wiig, both of whom cut their brewing teeth by making beer at home. Their approach is as uncompromising as the topography of the area, inflexible on using any ingredients that are not the best and determined to bring a wide range of quality beers to Norway. They knew what they didn't want: industrial-style, mass-produced lagers. Their challenge is to get their fellow countrymen to enjoy beers with taste.

The output from the brewery isn't large; production is still measured in hundreds of barrels rather than millions. But its influence is now becoming worldwide because the beers are exported to more than twenty countries.

Kjetil Jikiun and Gunnar Wiig wanted to set the highest possible standards for craft brewers. Their beers should be individual and use only the best ingredients, such as the famed Maris Otter English malt and fine hops such as Cascade, Centennial, Chinook and Columbus from the USA.

For those who dark beers deter, don't let the colour influence you. Black is beautiful and Nøgne Ø's stout is easy drinking. The rich flavours caress the palate rather than attack it. It looks quite beautiful in a glass. A dark body topped by a dark, almost brown, head. It is full of chocolate and coffee notes and a chorus of malt tastes with layers of dark fruits and vanilla.

In addition to its range of regular, seasonal and one-off beers, the brewery is one of the few places outside Japan that is making sake, fermented rice grain. Sticking to the company's uncompromising belief that only the best will do, the sake is made using an extended and precise fermentation, unlike most commercial sakes. Dogged yes, but only the best will do for Nøgne Ø.

24. THE POET
Style: Oatmeal stout
Strength: 5.2% ABV
Brewer: New Holland
Country of origin: USA
First brewed: 1999

'Once upon a midnight dreary, while I pondered, weak and weary', starts Edgar Allan Poe's poem 'The Raven'. Well a glass of New Holland's oatmeal stout would have lifted his mood. The American poet was at the forefront of the 'art for art's sake' movement and the architect of the modern

short story. Poe was fascinated by style and construction. In the same way, the brewers of New Holland care passionately about the provenance and quality of each of the ingredients they put into their beers.

New Holland's deep roots in the craft industry go back to 1997, when it opened its brewpub in Holland, Michigan. Malt and hops were their words and it was their task using art, craft and inspiration to transform these natural ingredients into great beers and then to share them with people.

Fred Bueltmann is the brewery's vice president and a certified beer cicerone. Known as the 'Beer Evangelist', he believes his job is much more than making and selling good beer; it is also about telling people about it. He believes educating people about beer is vital if the craft beer revolution is to continue to expand and he wants as many colleagues as is possible to also become accredited cicerones. The company's ethos is simple: they want to improve the lives of their customers.

And it is educating people about its beer The Poet that has brought many drinkers to enjoy an oatmeal stout, a style that for most of the last century was outside the experience of the majority of beer drinkers. When it was launched, it became an instant hit.

An oatmeal stout is a member of the stout family. The oatmeal adds a marvellous rich, silky mouthfeel to a beer. It was a popular ingredient in England in the 19th century, especially because it was considered to make beer even more nutritious. Usually the grain is added to the mash as malted rolled or flaked oats. The resultant beers tend to be sweeter than dry stouts and often have a silken, smooth texture.

The Poet is a dark rich black in colour and like the best oatmeal stouts it has a rich, creamy mouthfeel. The Nugget and Glacier hops give the beer a clear bitterness and aromatic notes of citrus and fruit. There are swathes of roasted barley, creamy chocolate and dark rummy fruit.

The cap on the brewery's bottles carries the slogan 'Art in Fermented Form'. This is a beer for contemplative sipping and for letting the imagination wander. It is best not to serve it too cold because this subdues the lovely aromas of the beer. A creamy epic beer, it really is poetry in a glass.

23. LONDON LAGER
Style: Lager
Strength: 4.5% ABV
Brewer: Meantime
Country of origin: UK
First brewed: 2010

A London lager. Surely there must be some mistake. London is better known as home of the beer-style porter and a place for brewing ales. And Guinness too, which was brewed in the capital at Park Royal for many years. But a lager?

Meantime brewmaster Alastair Hook spent twenty years planning the quintessential English lager. It was a labour of love. He learnt brewing skills at Heriot-Watt University in Edinburgh and the world-renowned Munich Technical University in Germany. There is not much he doesn't know about beer. His training, he says, taught him to respect the ingredients of beer and that only the best can be used to make fine beers.

He wanted to show that a light, zesty beer that is full of taste could be driven by the flavour of the barley and hops

© Meantime

rather than the yeast. That a beautifully created, simple beer could be made. In London. His reasoning was simple. The great European lager brewers use very soft water and neutral yeasts to ensure that only the flavours of their locally grown malt and hops come to the fore. English yeasts tend to produce fruitier flavoured beers.

Hook is on a mission to show that beer has real taste. A keen chronicler of the history of beer and its cultural importance, he wanted to show that a good lager was much more than chilled fizz. His philosophy for creating his lager was simple. If he could make it, it could well provide a stepping stone for leading drinkers on to more flavoursome beers. He also wanted to create a draught, unpasteurised, that could be drunk straight from a tank at the brewery, in the same way keller beers are sold in Germany. His ambition was to brew a properly lagered beer that allows the hops and malt in the beer to be fully expressed.

So put aside the notion that this beer is going to be high in fizz and low in taste. Hook chose good malting barley from East Anglia and some of the world's best hops from Kent. To lager a beer required it to be 'lagered' for a long period at a cool temperature. This helps bring out the characteristic flavours expected in a lager. London Lager is given a generous six weeks of conditioning before it is bottled. The best Bavarian lager brewers would give their lagers a similar ageing time. Some mass-market lagers are matured for a lot less than six days, let alone six weeks.

The draught version of the beer is sold as brewery fresh. It has proved to be a great success. The brewery fresh beer, unfiltered and unpasteurised, is put into a horizontal tank, which is delivered to a pub. The large tank is usually displayed so the customers can see it. Inside the tank is not just the beer, but a sealed bag of compressed air, which pushes the beer to the beer pump.

The beer pours a pale golden colour with a thin white head. The taste is clean, of biscuit malt, and the aromas are of fresh grass or even hay. Crisp and refreshing, it is a lager worthy of the finest beer garden. Hook's mantra of never compromising on quality has proved right.

22. DUCHESSE DE BOURGOGNE

Style: Flemish red ale
Strength: 6.2% ABV
Brewer: Verhaeghe Vichte
Country of origin: Belgium
First brewed: Early 1900s

Could this beer be the bridge between grain and grape? If anyone has a friend who says they don't like beer and only drink wine, this could be the drink for them. Don't serve it in a beer glass, but pour it into a favourite wine goblet. Marvel at its beguiling, ruby red, Burgundy hue. Enjoy the swirling red berry aromas and enjoy the sweet tart finish.

Brewers have probably been putting beer in wood barrels since they were first invented. But in recent times for most the wood was meant to be benign and impart no flavours to the beer. However, it is only wine and whisky makers and Belgian brewers who realised wood means flavour – great flavour.

Duchesse de Bourgogne is a beer from West Flanders, which is produced by a mixed fermentation of yeast and lactobacilli and then a long, gentle maturation in oak. The tannins in the oak give the beer its fruity character. After

© Verhaeghe-Vichte

two fermentations, the beer goes for maturation into the oak barrels for eighteen months. The final product is a blend of eight-month-old beer with eighteen-month-old beer. The average age of the Duchesse de Bourgogne before being bottled is one year. The result is a complex blend of acidic tartness and sherry flavours. It is with good reason that other brewers, from the USA to Japan, Italy and beyond, are trying to recreate the style. Worldwide, sour red beers are one of the hottest styles there are.

The beer was recently showcased at the British Guild of Beer Writers awards dinner and paired with a dish comprising smoked venison, goat's cheese and a terrine of fig and apple. According to the menu notes: 'The venison dish is über-complex with apple juice, fig sweetness, beetroot and red wine vinegar, smoke and cheese fattiness to deal with. An immediate flavour hook of acidity is needed to tie in, cut through and contrast. The Duchesse achieves this with its intensely fruity sourness balanced by aged oaky and malty flavours and spiciness.'

The beer's name comes from Mary the Duchess of Burgundy, who reigned over the Low Countries from 1477 until her death aged 25 in 1482 after a horse-riding accident. Her image can be seen on the beer's label.

The brewery also makes an interesting cherry beer called Echt Kriekenbier, using real fruit. It too is a blended Flemish red and comprises a mixture of one- and two-year-old cheery beers.

Verhaeghe Vichte is a small family-owned firm that started brewing in 1885. Once most of its production would have been sold in Brussels. Cases of the beer would have rattled into the city on the trains that run from Vichte. World wars nearly finished the brewery off, but both times it recovered, even though it was a slow and painful process. In the 1950s the beer became a regional novelty, little known outside its hinterland. However, slowly it became known outside of Belgium. Beer aficionados around the world got the sweet taste of sour.

21. DALE'S PALE ALE
Style: American pale ale
Strength: 6.5% ABV
Brewer: Oskar Blues
Country of origin: USA
First brewed: 1998

The canning of beer has an explosive history. Early efforts to put beer into metal containers weren't that successful. The American Can Co. began experimenting with canned beer in the 1900s. But the cans couldn't withstand the more than 5 bar pressure from carbonation – and exploded. It was back to the drawing board. However, by the end of Prohibition in 1933, the company had developed a technique that seemed to work.

Krueger's Cream Ale and Krueger's Finest Beer were the first beers sold to the public in a can. People loved them. Compared with glass bottles, the cans were lightweight, cheap, easy to stack and transport. The idea quickly spread and a small, relatively unknown Welsh brewer, Felinfoel, was the first in Europe to put a beer into a can. One of the criticisms then was that the taste of beer was tainted by the metal. But then Felinfoel hit on the idea of coating the inside of the cans with an inert wax. It was a shrewd move

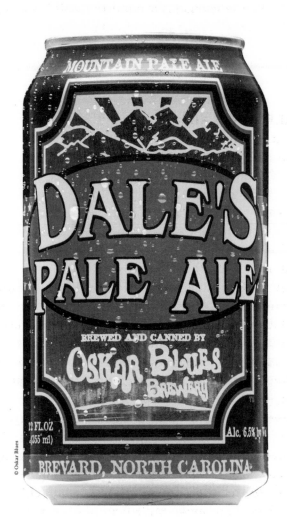

© Oskar Blues

because the family which owned Felinfoel also had a tinplate company in Llanelli, where cans could be made.

Over time the demand for cans grew and grew, but their reputation wasn't always positive among beer aficionados – cans were regarded as downmarket and only suitable for pile-it-high, sell-it-cheap beers in supermarkets. Convenient? Yes. Easy to dispose of? Yes. And the quality of the beer? Oh dear.

The Oskar Blues brewery was established in Lyons, Colorado, in 1998, and was among the first of a new wave of US brewpubs. The craft beer movement in the USA was starting to gain momentum. Its Dale's Pale Ale was well received; locally it rightly gained a good reputation for its assertive hop, orange peel citrus nose, floral blossom flavours underpinned by a good base of pale ale. It is a bitter beer too, and drinkers weaned on light American lagers often found the first bite of it on the palate was very aggressive. But once they acquired the taste for it, they loved it.

In 2002, Oskar Blues' founder Dale Katechis took the bold step of putting all his beers into cans. Quickly, he became a vocal advocate for canning beer, affirming that there would be no can taste. The richly flavoured canned Dale's Pale Ale benefits from the freshness-keeping power of aluminium cans. The recipe requires a lot of US hops, with big resiny and tropical flavours, which seem to sing from the can.

Drinkers loved the retro chic of the cans and the move certainly proved to be the right business decision as Oskar Blues has grown to become the largest American craft brewery to exclusively put beer in cans.

People got the taste for craft beer in cans, loving the idea that not only did the beer taste good, it was also easy to carry. And the can was easily recycled: a boon in an area where people loved the outdoor life and liked to hike or go mountain bike riding. As the brewery says: 'Cans keep beer fresher, longer by eliminating the damaging effects of light and ingressed oxygen while being infinitely recyclable and portable ... taking them where your next soul saving adventure takes you.'

Canning is growing in the UK too. Logan Plant, founder of Beavertown, said his bottle use is waning. 'I'm looking to push bottles out but for a few specialty beers. The acceptance of our cans has been amazing. Since we started up our canning line, cans have already become 65% of our sales, while bottles are just 7%.'

According to the Brewers Association (the US trade group for craft brewers), more than 10 per cent of America's nearly 3,000 small and independent craft brewers are now canning all or some of their beers. A US website, CraftCans.com, lists about 1,500 canned craft beers from 418 US craft breweries, in a wide array of different beer styles.

Cans are still explosive, not because they cannot take the pressure, but because canned beers are the fastest growing sector of the beer market.

20. TAP5 MEINE HOPFENWEISSE
Style: Bock
Strength: 8.2% ABV
Brewer: Schneider Weisse
Country of origin: Germany
First brewed: 2008

The brewers at Schneider Weisse are considered artists. But their palette is wheat and their canvas is beer. Its beers are renowned.

© Schneider Weisse

The family-owned brewer stands on the banks of the Danube some 110 km north-east of Germany's greatest brewing city Munich, in the heart of Bavaria. Its original home was Munich, but the site was destroyed in 1944 during the Second World War. So Schneider Weisse moved to its current home in Kelheim. However, its original site was rebuilt and it has now become a famed beer hall.

Since 1872, the brewery has been brewing a wheat beer. A weissbier is the classic wheat beer of Bavaria. They are usually characterised by having a yellowish hue, which comes from the mix of barley and wheat used in the grist. According to German law, a minimum of 50 per cent of the grist should be wheat; usually they will contain much more. They are often packaged unfiltered and have lots of cloudiness from the yeast.

Curiously, Bavaria is often regarded as one of the spiritual homes of bottom-fermented lagers, but a wheat beer is top fermented, often in open vessels. For most of the last century, sales of Bavarian wheat beers were declining and it was left to Schneider to keep the beer's cloudy flag flying. By the 1970s a revival in wheat beers began. The company was in the right place to reap the benefit of a revival in sales of wheat beer, which has now become the most popular style of beer in Bavaria.

Today, the brewery is run by the sixth generation of the Schneider family. Many regard its flagship beer as Unser Original, which is today known as TAP7 Mein Original. It's a classic wheat beer style. Amber coloured, it has a great white head and aromas of ripe bananas and cloves. But it is its TAP5 Meine Hopfenweisse that takes the brewery from the ordinary to the extraordinary. It's a doppelbock, a style that originated in Munich, and typically stronger than 7 per cent ABV.

German brewers are renowned for their conservative approach to the brewing of good beer. Many still believe in their so-called purity law the Reinheitsgebot, even though a weissbier technically violates the law. In doing so, some closed ranks and shut their minds to what was happening in the beer world, and then came the craft beer revolution. Their dogma was probably the downfall for many, for the beer world was changing.

Schneider Weisse was different and in 2007 it threw away the constraints of tradition and brewed a collaboration beer with one of the world's greatest brewers, Garrett Oliver of Brooklyn Brewery in New York. Together with Schneider Weisse's brewmaster Hans-Peter Drexler, Oliver created a Wagnerian symphony of a beer. It was a big, dry hopped doppelbock. Dry hopping means the addition of hops after boiling and fermentation have finished. The hops might be added to the fermenter, the conditioning tank or even the serving vessel. It is a cold fusion technique that adds intense aromatics to a beer. It is a style commonly used in Britain, but became very popular with the new wave of US craft brewers, who used American hops that were often characterised by their aromatic oils, which had been shunned for many years by European brewers.

TAP5 has an orange-yellow hue in the glass and aromas of tropical fruit. Flowery-flavoured Hallertauer and Sapphire hops are used together with a traditional grist of 50 per cent barley malt and wheat. The beer was originally brewed as a one-off, but it has now become a regular in Schneider's brewing stable.

The brewery is continuing to innovate and is experimenting with the barrel ageing of some of its beers.

19. STEAM BEER

Style: Steam beer
Strength: 4.9% ABV
Brewer: Anchor
Country of origin: USA
First brewed: 1971

Was this the beer that made the West?

Today, the name steam beer is a registered trade mark for Anchor Brewing, but in the late 1800s there were at least 25 breweries in San Francisco making a style called steam. Also, it seems likely that in the Golden State, California, there were many other brewers producing this style of beer.

At a time when tens of thousands of people had headed to California, lured by the dream that they could discover gold, beer of course came with them and a style developed that seemed to meld two great European brewing traditions, ale and lager. In an era before refrigerators, lager-style yeasts were fermented at warmer ale temperatures. The gold rush became the beer rush. Many believe the beer was called steam because of the high levels of carbonation the beer had, as it would gush when served in a bar.

Another theory for the name of the beer is that it was named after the steam that rose from the fermenting vessels and coolships when hot wort was poured in. The truth is probably out there somewhere, hiding in the steamy mists of time. However, whatever the truth is, refrigeration techniques were developed and the style fell out of favour as drinkers turn to chilled lagers.

The original Anchor brewery opened in 1874 as the Golden City Brewery. It became the Anchor Brewery in 1896 when it was bought by two German entrepreneurs. It was destroyed by the San Francisco earthquake in 1906 and rebuilt in a new location. Prohibition closed it, but it reopened in 1933, only to be razed by fire some months later. Phoenix-like, it rose again, but it never really flew until the heir to the Maytag washing machine empire bought a share of it in 1965.

Fritz Maytag had been told by restauranteur Fred Kun, owner of his favourite restaurant 'The Old Spaghetti Factory', that the brewer of his beer of choice was struggling and might close. Maytag decided he was going to save the brewery. Anchor was in a pretty parlous state when he became involved – hardly surprising, because it had suffered years of poor management.

At the time many local brewers were closing. They were being squeezed out of business by the onward march of the big national brewers. But Maytag was adamant he was going to retain the beer traditions of the brewery. He would not produce a beer that tasted the same as the others on sale. He became the sole owner of the brewery in 1969. He threw himself into his project and wanted to learn everything he could about brewing. He travelled to the UK to learn about beer styles and researched the origins of steam beer, a beer style that seemed to be unique to America.

In 1971, Maytag unveiled his own version of a steam beer, which he believed was close to the recipe of the beer produced before Prohibition. In the glass it is a gorgeous copper colour. The Northern Brewer hops add herbal and woody notes to the aroma. It is sweet on the tongue and has a clean, bittersweet finish. For many, Steam Beer became the gateway into the world of craft beer.

In its early days Maytag and the Anchor brewery were an inspiration for many aspiring craft brewers. In particular, his Liberty Ale, which is full of fruity and floral flavours and has

© Anchor

a crisp, entrancing bitterness on the palate, is still regarded as the benchmark for American pale ales. It was one of the first beers to use Cascade hops. The era of flavoured, aromatic hops with lots of citrus flavours had begun.

In 2010, Maytag sold the brewery to the Novato Group. He had decided it was time to retire. Maytag might not have discovered gold when he bought the Anchor brewery, but he has certainly given us some golden beers.

18. BUD B:STRONG

Style: Imperial pale ale
Strength: 7.5% ABV
Brewer: Budweiser Budvar
Country of origin: Czech Republic
First brewed: Unknown

Deep underground, beneath the Budvar brewery in the Czech Republic, there is a labyrinth of caves and cellars where the sun never shines. Here, where the temperature is rarely ever higher than 1°C and the brewery staff always seem to wear winter clothes, is where two, not just one, of the world's greatest beers are fermented and matured. It's a slow process, but then the best things in life should be worth waiting for.

Budvar's flagship beer Budweiser takes 100 days to reach perfection. Few beers in the world have the exquisite luxury of such a long conditioning. However, the brewery's imperial lager Bud B:Strong is given 200 long, cold days at near zero to mature.

The underground zero conditioning allows the taste and aroma of the beer to slowly develop. Imperial is a term often reserved for use by brewers making a beer for a crowned head of Europe. However, in recent years it has been taken by many US craft brewers and used to describe a beer that is stronger than usual. Anheuser-Busch, the US brewer of Budweiser, is sometimes described as the king of beers; however, it is doubtful that the Czech Bud has been brewed to honour the beers from US Budweiser's spiritual home of St Louis.

For many years, the two brewers have been in a fierce legal battle over the use of the trademark Budweiser. Once these legal actions were an inconvenience, but in an era of global brands and planet-wide ambitions, expansion in more than 40 markets is being hampered. The battle between Budvar and Anheuser-Busch is already a 100-year war with the companies clashing in and out of courts. Anheuser-Busch argues that Budvar was not launched until twenty years after the American brewer launched his Bud, but the Czechs contend that since the Samson brewery was operating in the town of Budweis since 1795, this is irrelevant.

The first attempt to settle the companies' differences was an agreement from 1911, in which Budvar's predecessor, Ceský akciový pivovar, gave its consent to the use of the Budweiser trademark by Anheuser-Busch, with the exception of its use in connection with the word Original, so that customers are not misled into believing that Anheuser-Busch's beer products come from Ceské Budejovice in the Czech lands. It is highly unlikely a beer drinker would be muddled by the incredibly popular light American lager and Budvar, but it is a row that has helped lawyers get rich for generations.

The soft water for Bud B:Strong is drawn from a well 300 metres under the brewery, where the water collected 10,000

© Budweiser Budvar

years ago. The barley used to make the beer is grown nearby; two Moravian varieties are used, Malz and Bojo. And the brewery is still an advocate for whole hop cones from the semi-early red-bine Saaz aromatic hops.

Once a year, the brewery makes a special version of Bud B:Strong, a tradition that began in 2013. Fresh, green, unripe hops are added to the beer. One early morning, as the sun is rising, usually in late August or early September, the hops are picked and rushed backed to the brewery to be added to a batch of Bud. Normally hops are dried before being used by a brewer, but by bypassing the kiln and coming straight from the bine to the brew house, delicate citrus flavours are added to the beer.

The bliss of a green-hopped beer is the aroma and flavour, which capture something of a dew-heavy sunlit summer's morning and add it to the beer. Budvar's unique yeast strain is then added to the hopped wort and fermentation begins. The southern Bohemian brewery has been using the same strain of yeast since 1895.

Once the initial fermentation is complete, the long process of maturation begins. The beer is to be conditioned in a closed tank. But before the beer is sealed into the tank, it is krausened. It's a process that was developed to enhance the flavours of the beer. A portion of fermented beer is added to the beer, restarting fermentation. The tank is then sealed so that the carbon dioxide created by the fermentation dissolves into the beer. This helps reduce any off flavours and puts a fresh zest into the beer.

Pale in colour, but not in character, Bud B:Strong is a fulsome beer. It has a good rounded mouthfeel and a long warming finish. It is a rock 'n' roll beer with the volume turned up to 11. The dark, golden liquid is topped by a dense, snow-white foam. The beer has a clear biscuit malt character. It's powerful, full bodied and graced by a fine hoppy aroma and notes of grassy spice.

17. UTOPIAS
Style: Strong ale
Strength: Varies; 27% ABV
Brewer: Samuel Adams
Country of origin: USA
First brewed: 2001

'Is this really a beer?' If you happen to be a judge at a beer competition and someone asks the question while adjudicating on the strong ale or speciality class, the chances are they could be blind-sampling Samuel Adams' Utopias. Yes, it is a beer. And it is stunning.

The Samuel Adams brewery has been wowing drinkers with its beers since it first produced Boston Lager in 1985. The brewery's name was taken to honour the American Revolution leader, who when he wasn't changing the political face of the world was also a maltster and brewer. Drinkers quickly fell in love with this bright, amber lager-style beer. Suddenly beer wasn't just yellow and didn't just have fizz, it had taste too.

At first the company was quite small, but now the company has grown to the point where it is big and nearly one in five craft beers drunk in the USA come from the brewery. But the brewery is much more than a one-trick pony. The good beers kept on coming. There was Double Bock, Irish Red, Latitude and many more.

But the company, which also runs a successful competition for its employees to develop new challenging beers, wanted to push the boundaries of beer. When Samuel Adams founder Jim Koch first brewed beer commercially, he said he wanted to offer American drinkers full-flavoured beers that were made in the USA. 'Over the years we have continued to push the boundaries of beers with extreme beers such as Samuel Adams Millennium and Infinium', said Koch. At 20 per cent ABV, Millennium is an ultra-strong barley wine. It is a strong beer, full of warm, woody notes. Infinium has a bit of a bubble to it and has a crisp champagne-like brew.

Koch was pushing the boundaries of beer, but he wanted to go further. He wanted to make a beer that would rival the world's finest ports, sherries and cognacs. Currently, Utopias at 27 per cent ABV is regarded as the strongest in America, though others worldwide claim to make a stronger brew: currently Brewmeister's Snake Venom, Schorschbräu's Bock and BrewDog's The End Of History, with strengths above 55 per cent ABV, are vying for this title.

A great beer has to start with the best ingredients. A supply of Noble hops was sourced – Hallertau Mittelfrüh, Spalt Spalter and Tettnang Tettnanger. To give the beer its required ruby black colour, a blend of Samuel Adams' two-row pale malt, Caramel 60 and Munich were put into the mash tun. And two of Samuel Adams' yeast strains were called into action, including its sparkling wine-style yeast. 'This extraordinary brew is the result of complex and carefully timed brewing processes. With each brew of Utopia, we release a completely new brew', said Koch.

Koch is insistent the beer's strength is created by brewing and not distillation or added spirit. Describing the 2013 brew, Koch says it is a blend of batches, some having been aged up to twenty years in a variety of barrels. 'We aged a portion of the beer in hand selected single use bourbon casks from the award winning Buffalo Trace distillery. This additional ageing process enhances the beer's distinctive vanilla and maple notes', said Koch.

To add to the virtuoso complexity of the brew, some of it was stored in former port casks, to add dark fruit aromas. And if that was not enough, some of the brewery's Kosmic Mother Funk (KMF) was tipped in. KMF is a wild ale that has been aged in Hungarian oak casks for at least twelve months. This adds an earthy sourness and red fruit notes of cherries and plums to the beer. And of course a special beer needs a special bottle. So it is put into a ceramic decanter modelled on one of the shapes of a traditional brewery copper kettle. 'The beer is extraordinary', said Koch.

Utopia might be an imagined place or state of things where everything is perfect. But add an 's' and you get Utopias, and there is nothing fictional about it. Try a glass of it and you really can let your imagination run riot. This beer is for real. 'It's the brewer's art at its finest', says Koch.

16. URBOCK
Style: Smoked beer/rauchbier
Strength: 6.5% ABV
Brewer: Schlenkerla
Country of origin: Germany
First brewed: Unknown

If you love beer, then the beautiful baroque island city of Bamberg, on the banks of the River Regnitz and the

© Schlenkerla

Main-Donau canal in Upper Franconia, Bavaria, has to be a must visit destination. This stunning medieval city is home to eleven great breweries and the greatest of them all is Schlenkerla.

Many of Bamberg's beers have a smoky secret, rauchbier. To make beer, a cereal, usually barley or wheat, is malted, which means that the process of germination is started. This begins the process of releasing the essential sugars needed by the brewer. To stop the germination going too far, the growing grain is then stopped through the application of heat, which dries it.

In the early days of malting, the drying would be done using wood fires. These were difficult to manage and often the malt would be burnt and its flavour tainted by the smoke. The development of coke in the 19th century gave maltsters the ability to control the heat, and resulted in a lighter and cleaner tasting malt.

In Bamberg, tourists visiting the cathedral are told a story of how a fire, hundreds of years ago, once burnt down a wooden cloister. The conflagration tainted the flavour of some malt stored in an adjacent brew house. A brewer went on to use the fire-damaged grain and discovered that it gave the beer a special smoky flavour, for which many beers in Franconia are now renowned. Before the developments of modern malting, possibly all beers had a smoky hue.

The Schlenkerla brewpub is close to the cathedral, where the unlikely tale of the providential fire is told. The pub dates back to the 15th century. Once brewing did take place here, but today it happens a short walk away. Today, malt in the Schlenkerla malthouse is still smoked over a beechwood fire, which imparts marvellous wood fire, peaty textures to the finished beers. The current owner is Matthias Trum, who is the sixth generation of his family to run the brewery. He is passionate about keeping the brewing of rauchbier alive.

The name Schlenkerla is Bamberg slang for someone who swings his arms while walking in a shuffling manner. It's not an easy image to visualise. Trum said: 'Schlenkerla dates back to the year 1405; I myself am the brewmaster and the sixth generation of my family to work here.' He is adamant that the original Schlenkerla, the man with the shuffling walk, was one of his ancestors. He continued: 'The Urbock smoked beer, like the classic Märzen smoked beer, have been brewed by my family as long as we can remember. There are no records as to when, or why it was brewed the first time. Presumably it's been around since the start of the brewery.'

And where better to enjoy rauchbier than the brewery's pub. The warmth of its world famous smoky beers is as warm as the welcome. Tables are often shared and strangers strike up conversations. Good beer is a fantastic social lubricant. The smoked beer is also a perfect partner to the robust Bavarian dishes on the menu, including onions stuffed with beery meatballs and fulsome hocks of ham.

The Urbock is one of the brewery's smoky seasonal beers, which is usually only sold in October. Dark brown in colour, it is topped by a dark, creamy head and exudes a spicy, smoky nose. Its flavours of burnt wood and ham are balanced by sweeter malt flavours and dried fruit. The mouthfeel is big and there is a long roasted, smoky finish. It's a special beer.

But Trum doesn't just live in the past, producing a beer from a long-ago era. He is also developing new beers using his unique malt. The brewery makes a stunning doppelbock called Eiche (oak, in German) with the barley malt smoked over burning oak, giving the beer a softer character than the spicy beechwood, and a smoky wheat beer made with smoked barley and wheat.

Rauchbier might not be to everyone's taste, but the opportunity to try one should never be allowed to go up in swirls of smoke.

15. BEER GEEK BREAKFAST
Style: Stout
Strength: 7.5% ABV
Brewer: Mikkeller
Country of origin: Denmark
First brewed: 2005

A breakfast beer? US President Barack Obama is said to have enjoyed a crisp, cold weissbier for breakfast at a recent G7 summit. Clearly, he was following a presidential tradition, because President George Washington and the founding father of the USA, Benjamin Franklin, both refer in their diaries to drinking beer, Franklin specifically so at breakfast.

Once it would have been commonplace to drink a beer for breakfast. Very weak, the beer was, and sometimes still is, made from the 'second running' of a stronger beer's mash. Known as small beer, it would often be given to children, and some workers would receive more than five litres a day to keep them hydrated. And who could blame them? Water was often too dangerous to drink, but very weak beer, the water of which had been boiled in the brewing process, was much safer and it was nutritious too. Look back through English literature and from Geoffrey Chaucer to William Shakespeare, and Thackeray's *Vanity Fair*, people drank beer for breakfast.

But one of 7.5 per cent ABV, that would be a bit strong even for the most hardened drinker. Innovative, imaginative and just a little bit weird, Mikkeller has brought soul, and in the spirit of American micros, rule breaking to the staid Danish brewing scene. Its boldness has won it worldwide recognition for its life-affirming brews.

A teacher-turned-master, Mikkel Borg Bjergsø is a modern-day prince of Denmark. But his story is no Shakespearean tragedy. The only revenge that Bjergsø exacted was on the rule book for brewing beer. He just destroyed it. He has turned a classroom experiment into one of the most innovative breweries in the world. But until recently there were no bricks and mortar to his brewery. He is a nomad, a travelling troubadour. This has seen him journey to craft brewers worldwide, people who share his passion for emotion, excitement and creating agitation in the world of beer, to brew. His travels have taken him to England, Scotland, the USA, Belgium, Norway and, of course, his home country of Denmark.

With his then business partner Kristian Klarup Keller, he decided to construct an oatmeal stout. It was their first commercial beer. Throughout their years of home brewing they had been experimenting with the attributes of different malts. The trials with the structure of the beer at first were disappointing, something was missing. What could it be? Coffee? Percolators were bought, coffee beans were sourced. Hours were spent talking to other brewers and brewing the coffee needed to add extra flavouring. And now on brewing days the brewery isn't filled with the sweet, nutritious aromas of malt being mashed but of coffee being boiled.

It is a beer heavy with intensity, which is held together by a precarious balance of roasted barley dark malts and coffee flavours and the refreshing wave of citrus flavours from the American Cascade and Centennial hops.

© Mikkeller

And now the company without a brewery plans to double its production when the brewery Mikkeller Brewing in San Diego, California, opens. 'We are extremely excited and it will certainly be fun to open our first physical brewery and present Americans with the beer we have brewed over there', said Bjergsø. 'The USA is our second largest and potentially our largest market. Currently, we brew most of our beer in Belgium and Norway, which is then shipped to the USA. This acquisition gives us an opportunity to expand in the American market, because we can brew on equal terms with American breweries. Our beer can be fresher, and we save on shipping costs.'

The San Diego brewery was previously owned by Alesmith, which sold the brewery so they could fund an expansion. Many interested buyers contacted Alesmith, which instead chose to contact Mikkeller, because they believed that the Danish microbrewery would be able to contribute something new and fun to the beer scene in California and thus draw more beer lovers to the area.

And what were journalists offered to drink at the early morning conference to announce the opening of the brewery? Beer Geek Breakfast, of course. The fun just keeps coming.

14. LA FOLIE
Style: Sour brown ale
Strength: 6% ABV
Brewer: New Belgium
Country of origin: USA
First brewed: 2000

Great beer, and it's all about wood.

A lot of bikes stand outside the New Belgium brewery in Fort Collins, Colorado. And many cycling references feature in the names of the brewery's beers, including Slow Ride, Shift and Fat Tire. They seem appropriate because the founder of the New Belgium brewery, Jeff Lebesch, was inspired to open his own brewery in 1991 following a cycle tour of Belgium.

La Folie, French for 'the folly', is a beer steeped in New Belgium brewing tradition. The beer created quite a storm when it won gold at the Great American Beer Festival in 1997. There wasn't even a class for this style of beer. But the judges were wowed.

Now, New Belgium brewmaster Peter Bouckaert, a native Belgian who used to work at Rodenbach, says there must be seven classes for sour beers at the Great American Beer Festival. And he is dismissive of any craft brewer who doesn't have a programme for ageing beer in wood. 'Who are you?' he challenges. He believes that New Belgium is at the forefront of rediscovering the classic tastes of beers, before industrial production began a hundred or so years ago and encouraged most producers to move to single-culture yeasts. Now he is a curator for a 'zoo' of hundreds of lactobacillus, pediococcus and other bacteria.

© New Belgium

Lactobacillus and pediococcus are the two main bacteria that contribute sourness or acidity to a beer. Lactobacillus can ferment with or without oxygen and produce lactic acid, instead of alcohol, and carbon dioxide. Unwanted by most brewers, who shun the off flavours that can include a butterscotch or buttery flavour from diacetyl, they are an important component of sour beers. Pediococcus, which is the bug that helps turn cabbage into sauerkraut, ferments glucose into lactic acid but doesn't produce carbon dioxide. It adds rich complexity to a beer. Different barrels will progress in a different way. The skill of the sour beer brewers and blenders is to take the characteristics of different base beers to create the acid profile they are looking for.

Beneath the Fort Collins brewery there are now 64 large French oak foeders, large barrels, making it one of the most comprehensive wood beer programmes in the world. Here matures the beer that will be used for blending each beer. The staff call the room the foeder forest.

Wineries retire their foeders for a variety of reasons, but usually it is because the tannin flavours in the wood have been exhausted. Tannin is regarded as an essential flavour component of many wines. However, tannin is not a flavour brewers are usually looking for, so they are happy to take on the second-hand barrels, which as well as being perfect for storing beer are also excellent homes for microbes and wild yeasts.

The wood-aged La Folie spends from one to three years in oak barrels. Many American brewers of craft beers refer to their bacteria as critters and relish the opportunity of getting to know their barrel characteristics before blending with them. La Folie needs to be sharp and sour. It should have notes of fresh Granny Smith apples, cherry and plum skins. It will pour a dark mahogany into the glass, and on tasting it is a curious harmony of smooth and puckering.

In a twist on its sour beer theme, the brewery collaborated with five other brewers to produce several new beers to celebrate its 25 years of brewing. The Riff-Pack features collaboration brews all 'riffing' on New Belgium's popular Fat Tire Amber Ale. Each brewery, in collaboration with brewers from New Belgium, put their own unique spin on it. The riffers include Allagash, Avery, Firestone Walker, Hopworks Urban and Rhinegeist.

Allagash produced a version of the beer using a Belgian yeast sourced from the Poperinge region. Avery focused on a fruitier hop bill also with a dose of brett yeast. Firestone Walker created a west coast interpretation of Fat Tire with an assertive hop profile and a light lager yeast. Hopworks Urban created a tart Fat Tire bringing in apple and lactobacillus to help highlight that beautiful green apple snap inherent to the original Fat Tire and Rhinegeist has transformed Fat Tire into a Belgian strong ale, combining a fruity Belgian yeast strain with bready-sweet European and Colorado malts.

New Belgium's beers are no follies, they are the real deal.

13. 60 MINUTE IPA
Style: American IPA
Strength: 6% ABV
Brewer: Dogfish Head
Country of origin: USA
First brewed: 2003

One of the first US beer styles to evolve in the 1980s was the American pale ale. The earliest variants were derived from

English recipes but using American ingredients, particularly aromatic hops, which had long since been rejected by European brewers. American brewers didn't discover hops with flavours of citrus or blackcurrant. But they did use them. In handfuls. The late addition of hops helps to define the style of an American ale – they add a gale of aromatic flavours.

Sam Calagione, founder of Dogfish Head, likes to create bigger, bolder beers. He set up his brewery in a brewpub in Rehoboth Beach, Delaware, in 1995. It was Delaware's first brewpub and the smallest commercial brewery in America. Its very first batch, Shelter Pale Ale, was brewed on a system that essentially was three little kegs with propane burners underneath. Brewing 12-gallon batches of beer for a whole restaurant proved to be more than a full-time job. When the doors to the pub first opened, it brewed three times a day, five days a week.

One benefit to brewing on such a small system was the ability to try out a myriad of different recipes. Calagione quickly got bored brewing the same things over and over – that's when he started adding all sorts of weird ingredients and getting kind of crazy with the beers. He likes to make extreme beers, where he pushes the tastes and textures. His beers are not for the faint hearted.

Calagione is widely regarded as one of the most creative of the US craft brewers. He started brewing at home, before he founded the Dogfish Head Brewery in Milton, Delaware. It was here he developed his ideas for beers that use unusual ingredients or extreme amounts of traditional ingredients. He said: 'We make off-centred ales for off-centred people. That's what we do here at Dogfish Head. Whether its odd ingredients or crazy, made-up styles, you can be sure that a beer from Dogfish will challenge your perceptions of what beer is supposed to be.'

One of his weirdest brews was a recreation of a South American drink, called chicha, which is made with maize, peppercorns and fruit. To release the fermentable material in the ingredients, they have to be chewed and spat. The saliva is then collected and rolled into flattened cakes and dried in the sun. Enzymes in the saliva break down the starch in the maize to release the sugars necessary for fermentation; also the chewing helps sterilise the sugars in the cake, stopping them being spoiled by wild yeasts and bacteria. When he made his own version of chicha, Calagione said it took six people all day to chew and spit their way through three kilograms of Peruvian blue corn.

No spitting is involved in the creation of his 60 Minute IPA. According to Calagione, it is his ground zero beer, the company's best seller and his session beer for 'hard core hopheads'. Following mashing, the wort is boiled for an hour and every minute of the boil a slew of Northwest hops is added, in what seems like a continuous process. A rig comprising a bucket full of hops, which is vibrated by the electronics from a former computer football game, is used.

The beer's orange citrus character can be smelled as soon as a bottle is opened. It pours orange into a glass, and floral and piney flavours can be detected. But this is no hop-flavoured alcopop: there is a clear malt base underpinning and balancing it all.

In the early days of the brewery, Calagione once rowed eighteen miles to deliver a consignment of the beer to New Jersey. 'It was a long strange trip and it hasn't ended.'

12. PILSNER URQUELL
Style: Pilsner
Strength: 4.4% ABV
Brewer: SABMiller
Country of origin: Czech Republic
First brewed: 1842

Often mimicked, but rarely bettered, this has to be one of the best beers in the world.

Pilsener, pilsner or pils are the names often given to the most famous lager style in the world. And the spiritual birthplace of what is claimed to be the world's first bright golden beer is the city of Pilsen in Bohemia, in the Czech Republic.

Back in 1842, Bavarian brewer Josef Groll, working for the Plzeň brewing cooperative, brewed the first batch of what came to be known as pilsner beer. Up until then, Czech beers were probably cloudy and brown in colour. A master brewer, Groll was asked by Martin Stelzer, founder of the Burgher's Brewery of Pilsen, to brew a beer that was equal to the new style of copper-coloured, clear beers being developed in Vienna.

The beer was not the first golden beer, as is often claimed. The first golden beers came from England and were known as pale ales. Brewers in Bavaria were next to learn how to brew with pale malts. And it was this skill Groll brought with him to Plzeň. The beer he brewed became the pattern for a style of beer that has been brewed worldwide and probably accounts for more than nine out of ten of every beers brewed on the planet. Today, many brewers try to cut corners when making a lager, but these mass-produced beers that dominate the world beer market are pale imitations of a

true lagered beer. Time is needed to develop the clean, crisp flavours and assertive hop characteristics that are essential characteristics of the style.

Groll brought Bavarian yeast with him to Pilsen, as well as a team of brewing and barrel-making assistants. He created a fresh, clear, golden beer, topped with a wispy, snow-white head. The beer was perfect for serving in the recently developed clear glassware that was becoming very popular with drinkers.

The golden crystal clarity of the beer was made possible by advances in malting, which were being widely used elsewhere in Europe. The use of coke rather than hot coals, and hot air rather than direct heat, had made it much easier for maltsters to produce paler shades of malt.

Cold fermented, the beer abounds with sweet flavours from the Bohemian or Moravian barley and spicy Zatec hops, often known by their German name Saaz. The Saaz hops impart an especially fresh herbal aroma and contribute to a certain and classy finish. Lower in alcohol than many beers brewed at the time, the unfermented sugar in the beer contributes to its assertive richness.

The golden ale-style beers from Burton on Trent in England owe their success to the local supply of water that is high in salts, creating ideal conditions for the warmer fermenting ale yeasts to thrive. The Pilsner Urquell brewery takes its low sulphite, low carbonate water from its own springs, which through serendipity are ideal for pilsner production. The brewery was built on the bank of the Radbuza River, directly above a sandstone foundation that was easily carved with tunnels for cold storage, or lagering, of the beer.

Once the beer was fermented in large open vessels made of Bohemian oak. The brewery had more than 1,000 of them, each capable of holding more than 30 hectolitres.

The scale of the fermentation vessels was matched by a maze of underground galleries containing more than 3,500 large pitch-lined oak casks, where slowly, slowly in the cold, damp conditions the beers matured from a callow brew to one with a rich fullness.

Today, the wooden vessels have been replaced by the elegance and efficiency of steel and refrigeration. Pilsner Urquell's current head brewer Baclav Berka is only the sixth man in Urquell's history to hold this title. His father worked in the Urquell brewery too, so it's something of a family business for him. He is adamant his predecessor Josef Groll would have used steel rather than wood had it been available.

Drinking unfiltered pilsner in its home town, underneath the brewery, has to be one of the great experiences of any beer drinker. The highlight of a tour is to walk through dimly lit, ice-cool sandstone cellars, where unfiltered and non-pasteurised Pilsner Urquell poured straight from the conditioning tank can be tried. It is just perfection in a glass.

11. CRU BRUOCSELLA

Style: Lambic
Strength: 5% ABV
Brewer: Cantillon
Country of origin: Belgium
First brewed: 1998

Who says Belgium is boring? The country is the traditional home to more historic beer styles that are still being brewed than any other. One such is the palate-challenging lambic.

© Cantillon

A sour wheat-style beer exclusively brewed in and around the Brussels area, its fermentation mirrors medieval or even earlier brewing techniques. Just take a look at old Flemish paintings by artists such as Pieter Bruegel: many have earthenware jugs on the table that contained lambic beer.

It was a beer style first brewed before we understood about pure yeast strains – it was Louis Pasteur and Emil Hansen who developed this technology in the second half of the 19th century. With this understanding came the ability to brew consistent clean-tasting beers that were less likely to spoil. Despite this, the brewing of lambic beer has remained an ongoing and intriguing activity in the part of Brussels known as Payottenland.

At the heart of the style is a complex fermentation using naturally occurring wild yeasts and bacteria. The yeasts hang in the air, reside in the walls and can be found in the wooden rafters of Payottenland breweries; they are part of the fabric of the area. It is said that each lambic brewer has their own unique variation of the yeast and brews their own unique version of the style.

No beer traveller to Brussels should leave the city without visiting the Cantillon brewery and museum. Founded by Paul Cantillon in 1900, it was one of hundreds of breweries in the capital. Then there were many similar breweries in the area, brewing one of the world's great beer curiosities. Today, Cantillon's current owner Jean-Pierre Van Roy says it is hard for him to sell his beers in Brussels. But what is Belgium's loss is America's gain for 50 per cent of his beer is now exported. A telling map on the wall in the brewery shows what many small specialist beer producers in Belgium have had to do to survive: export. The map shows more than 30 places in the USA where people can go and buy lambic beers but only eleven in Brussels.

Here in the brewery, close to the Gare du Midi, and still using equipment that was installed in 1900, can be experienced the life-affirming joy of seeing beers brewed by spontaneous fermentation in an open vessel, before they are matured for long months in old oak casks, which lie in the brewery's basement.

The beer is a mixture of organic raw wheat (35 per cent) and malted barley (65 per cent). Three-year-old English hops (5 grams per litre of beer) are used. Most brewers use freshly dried hops for their aromatic, bittering and preservative qualities. However, lambic brewers only want the hops for their preservative qualities.

Once the beer has been boiled for several hours with the hops, it is pumped into an open vessel called a coolship. Here the wort cools quickly. The coolship is close to the ceiling and there are vents and holes in the wall and the roof through which fresh air and the area's wild yeast flow, caressing and infecting the beer.

After fermentation, the Grand Cru Bruocsella is matured for three years in oak barrels. Van Roy says he is the servant to and not the master of the beer. The contents of each cask are unique, an age-old exploration of how beer's simple ingredients of grain, hops and wild yeast can evolve and develop their own character.

For the uninitiated palate the first taste of a Cantillon beer can be a startling experience. It's tart, bitter, acidic and tongue curling. But give it time. Use all your senses to explore every facet of these historic beers. Many experience a Damascene moment and realise these are great and unique beers.

Many lambics are blended, but not Grand Cru Bruocsella, even though Van Roy is a skilled blender. It is more like a combination of wine and cider than what most of us recognise as a beer.

It is a beer that partners well with many foods – it is not to be drunk quickly but savoured, in wine not beer glasses. It is an aristocratic beer, dry in character with a discreet but underlying acidity. It is a beer that will change over time, developing different nuances and qualities.

And Van Roy wants to keep brewing the beer for many more years, but he is fearful that global warming may halt production. The brewing of his beloved lambics is seasonal. Fermentation takes place during the cooler autumn evenings from October onwards. On some occasions recently temperatures were too warm and production had to be halted.

It would be a tragedy if the world's rising temperatures saw an end to this great beer.

10. XYAUYÙ
Style: Barley wine
Strength: 14% ABV
Brewer: Baladin
Country of origin: Italy
First brewed: 2004

There are brewers in Italy? Indeed, there are. The country that is at the heart of wine culture and produces millions of bottles of vino also has an important part to play in beer culture.

From ancient Rome until the present, people in Italy have brewed beer. Today, it has a thriving craft brewing scene with more than 800 craft brewers making some of the most creative and interesting beers in the world. And one of the most exciting champions of the craft brewing scene is Teo Musso of Baladin. He is a man who is determined to change people's opinion of beer. Beer is not bland; it is not a yellow liquid intended to be drunk without care or thought. Beer is an experience as magical as listening to an aria or viewing a painting by a grand master.

Teo Musso's canvas is a brewery and bar in Piozzo, a small village high up in the Piedmont hills above Asti and Barolo wine country. He is tall, languid, studiously unkempt: the rock 'n' roll impresario of the beer world. His enthusiasm is infectious. His desire is to show that flare, creativity and individuality can create great beers. His beers are eclectic and experimental and a challenge to many people's perceptions of what a beer should be.

He is on a mission to show that beer can have a uniquely Italian twist. If you want to change the world, don't do it with sadness, do it with joy, says Carlo Petrini, founder of the Slow Food movement. It is this philosophy that Teo Musso brings to beer. His beers are joyous explorations of the tastes, textures and colours that can be created by the ingredients of beer. Some might find that flair overwhelms technical skill. And yes, some of the beers are challenging – but if you want bland, go and drink an industrial lager.

Teo Musso has a calling, indeed it's his vocation for beer to take centre stage while wine is sent to stand in the shadows. His creations are as much fine art as craft and science. One of his beers is made with unmalted kamut, an ancient wheat variety, which is laden with ginger and orange zest. A touch of myrrh provides a balsamic bitterness. Another is laced with citrus and spice, but the vibrancy of the curaçao and coriander is softened by the fruit flavours of figs and poached pears.

© Baladin

Xyauyù is an extraordinary beer. As it says on the sell-by date message on its label, 'to be consumed by the end of the world'. Xyauyù starts as a living, top-fermented beer. It is a barley wine; most do not have enough alcohol to approach the strength of a wine, but this beer does. The beer heritage comes from the British farmhouse tradition of brewing a strong beer for consumption by the wealthy. These beers often would be aged in wood for a year or more. They were often consumed in England when, because of war or other difficulties, wine imports from France were curtailed. It is a style that was revived by the new wave of craft brewers in the USA in the 1970s and was taken to another level at Baladin.

Xyauyù isn't just laid down for a long time; it is given eighteen months in a tank outside the brewery. The vented tank allows the air of the Langhe area to come into contact with the beer. This process oxidises the brown beer and creates a complex chorus of challenging flavours. Most people would say this would ruin a beer. However, slow and graceful oxidation adds complex Madeira flavours to a beer. This long treatment brings out swirling sherry flavours. It sits very still and brooding in a glass. The result is a complex, rich, nutty beer with aromas of raisins, prunes and well-polished old furniture. The aroma is intense with swathes of dried fruit and clamouring notes of sherry.

The line between genius and eccentricity is probably narrow. Teo Musso likes to plays music to some of his beers. A large set of headphones is attached to one of his fermenting tanks. He believes that the different rhythms of a piece of music will affect how the yeast performs. One composer has even written a piece of music specifically for him, for playing at different stages of a fermentation.

So what was the music played to the fermenting Xyauyù? Given the complexity of this beer, it was probably Stravinsky or Benjamin Britten. Both composers create musical works of astounding complexity that exude primitive, earthy and even atavistic tones. Their music is thrilling and compelling, yet they only use the same notes as all other composers, just like all brewers start with the same four notes – cereal, hops, malt and yeast.

If this is going to be my last drink, then I'm looking forward to the end of the world. Challenging yes, interesting certainly, and memorable? Undoubtedly.

9. DEUS BRUT
Style: Sparkling ale
Strength: 11.5% ABV
Brewer: Bosteels
Country of origin: Belgium
First brewed: 2000

Beer is an affordable luxury that can be enjoyed by everybody, and one of the most luxurious is Bosteels' DEuS. It is a beer that should be shared with friends and sipped from tall fluted glasses, to enhance the dancing of the bubbles within this extraordinary ale. Many beers claim to be godly blessed. However, DEuS is truly a sparkling, divine experience.

The beer's name pays homage to the Latin phrase 'dues for God'. It is a complicated beer to create. It starts life at Bosteels' family brewery in the village of Buggenhout in East Flanders. The beer is as classy and stylish as the brewery, which looks more like a stately home than a brewery. It is a fabulous palace of beer, which is run by the seventh

generation of the founding family. But to make the beer, the brewer first bottom ferments it with an ale yeast. Next a French twist is added to the Belgian base. The beer undergoes a process known as method champenoise, which is usually used to produce sparkling wines.

The process for bottling champagne was probably developed in England in the 1700s, when large barrels of French wine were imported that still contained some yeast. If the bottles weren't strong enough or the process was mishandled, they'd explode. In the case of DeuS Brut, the beer travels to Epernay in the Champagne region of France, where a champagne yeast is added and the beer is bottled with a metal crown cap. The beer then starts to re-ferment in the bottle and after standing upside down for three weeks, the sediment collects in the neck above the cap. As with a good sparkling wine, the bottles are placed in pupitres, or stillages, where they are turned around and brought from a horizontal into a vertical position. A turn is made several times a day to rouse the beer and sediment. After a time, the bottles will be stood upright. All the sediment formed during re-fermentation has gathered in the neck of the bottle, which will subsequently be disgorged.

The bottles are then fed into a machine which freezes the neck and turns the sediment into a lump of ice. The crown cap is removed and the pressure from the beer forces the ice out of the bottle, a process known as disgorging. A traditional cork is then put on the bottle, which is stored and carefully turned for at least nine months. The resultant exuberant beer is spicy, dry with hints of fruit and has bubbles that dance on the tongue. It is a beautifully clear, pale, sparkling beer, topped with a light snow-white head.

Its aroma is effervescent with some notes of fresh blossom and ginger. This must be the perfect aperitif. The finish is beautifully dry with a bare hint of delicate, spicy leather.

Would I want a glass of champagne to celebrate birthday, wedding or other special occasion? No, give me a glass of DeuS Brut every time; it's stunning.

8. IMPERIAL EXTRA DOUBLE STOUT
Style: Imperial stout
Strength: 9% ABV
Brewer: Harveys
Country of origin: UK
First brewed: 1998

There is something of the night about a glass of black beer. It is a dark, bold beer and it is a sip of history in a glass; brewery historian Peter Mathias described it as 'the first beer technically suited for mass production at contemporary standards of control'.

In 1998 an American importer approached a UK agency to source an authentic version of A. Le Coq's famed Imperial Extra Double Stout, which was first brewed in London and then at the Tartu brewery in Estonia, for sale in St Petersburg, Russia. It was to Harveys brewery in Sussex they turned.

Harveys' head brewer, Miles Jenner, said: 'Barclay Perkins Brewery supplied their Extra Stout to a Belgian merchant called Albert Le Coq. He, in turn, bottled it under his own label and shipped it to the Baltic regions – including St Petersburg and other Russian cities. A well-judged gift of five thousand bottles to the Russian military hospitals of Catherine the Great was rewarded with an Imperial Warrant of Appointment and Imperial Extra Double Stout was born. Later Le Coq was invited by the Tsarist government to brew this legendary beer within the Russian Empire and in 1912 production commenced in Tartu, the former province of Livonia, now Estonia. The brewery remains in existence, but production of their original brand has long ceased.'

To research the recipe, Jenner consulted his company's brewing records from the 1830s. 'I was struck by the lack of standard formulations in those days. The proportion of malts varied dramatically from brew to brew and yeast strains were freely exchanged between one local brewer and another. I concluded that public expectations were not particularly demanding.'

The Tartu brewery was as helpful as it could be, but wasn't precise. So Jenner turned to the recollections of the generation of brewers who had produced Barclay Perkins Russian Stout in London in the 1950s.

A recipe was devised, using a combination of two-thirds pale ale and one-third coloured malts: a combination of amber, brown and black. This was supplemented with invert sugar in the copper, which ultimately contributed 15 per cent of raw materials by weight and around 20 per cent of the wort composition. And then came the hops – lots of them. For every barrel of stout brewed, the hop weight was seven times higher than the company's famed Best Bitter.

The American importer was champing at the bit for the beer and, after nine months' storage by Harveys, it reached New York in March. The importer was ecstatic: 'Just a quick note to tell you that we are delighted at the aroma, flavour and taste profile. As we wished so much, even some tart/sour undercurrents can be tasted. We certainly do not want you to change anything in the recipe. Leave everything as is.'

© Harveys

It was launched at the historic Russian Tea Rooms in New York and got good reviews. *Ale Street News* wrote, 'Massive nose and flavour – liquorice, pomegranate, currants, prunes, toffee, celery, molasses, spare ribs. What isn't in this beer? So complex you can find almost anything.'

In England, one panel of brewing experts were a little more reserved: 'An intense flavour which is complex and distinctive. The roast, alcoholic and spicy notes combine in this unusually sweet and sour beer.'

All was going well until four months later, in July, when Jenner became aware that some of the Imperial Extra Double Stout bottles that had left the brewery had corks which were slowly rising up the neck of the bottle to be restrained by the foil capsule and that releasing this had an effect akin to discharging a champagne cork.

'The majority of the bottling was residing 3,500 miles away in a country that is not averse to litigation and I was concerned to put it mildly. By the end of the year we were getting a few reports of near misses but, thankfully, survived to tell the tale', said Jenner. 'Upon reflection, we should have heeded the fact that Georgian brewers and, indeed, Barclay Perkins, had apparently held their stouts for twelve months rather than the nine we had afforded. At any rate, we had brewed another batch and refilled our tanks shortly after the trial brew had been bottled. We kept an eye on this but little appeared to be happening. In fact, a volcano was smouldering; after what one might call a pregnant pause of nine months, the beer sprang to life and underwent a startling secondary fermentation. At its height we were releasing 30 lbs of pressure off the tanks overnight. When it had exhausted itself we decided to sample the beer and send it to BRI for analysis.'

It became apparent that alongside Harveys' depleted yeast strain was a healthy population of wild yeast, which looked very similar to its house yeast. 'I can tell you little about it except that it was first isolated on mushrooms in the 1920s and is often found in salty environments', said Jenner. It seems that after the Harveys yeast had stopped working, the wild yeast, which Jenner assumes was present in very low numbers within his yeast strain, comes into its own and, after a lengthy lag phase, kicks in to dramatic effect.

For all the worry, the 1999 vintage exceeded all expectations and won a gold medal at the Brewing Industry International Awards. Subsequent vintages of the beers were kept conditioned for a longer period of time and, rather than being put in a corked bottle, a metal crown top was used; gone was the fear of exploding corks.

Clearly it has worked as the beer has, so far, been the winner of a national or international award every year since it was first brewed by Harveys.

7. SORACHI ACE
Style: Saison
Strength: 7.6% ABV
Brewer: Brooklyn Brewery
Country of origin: USA
First brewed: 2009

One of the most beguiling of people to talk about beer is the brewmaster at New York's Brooklyn Brewery, Garrett Oliver. Garrett Oliver is an epicure – he likes the best things in life, and he does like good wine, but he is on a mission to show

© Brooklyn Brewery

that beer is the perfect partner to food and that it is time for wine to leave centre stage.

He loves nothing better than talking about beer. Well, that is unless he is talking about pairing beer with cheese. It is all about flavour and passion. Beer pairs so well with cheese. It is so much better than wine. Cheese coats the tongue with its covering of salt and fat. Wine cannot cut through this and its flavours are lost. But bubbly beer, with its mildly acidic carbonation, will break through the cheese barrier, releasing a kaleidoscope of flavours. The two become one and the sum of the parts is much bigger than if each was tasted on its own.

At a tasting some years ago at the famed White Horse pub in Parsons Green, West London, Oliver conducted a masterclass in beer and cheese tasting. For many years the pub was the haunt of the famed beer writer Michael Jackson. The pub was then run by Mark Dorber, who was part of a movement that took big, bold strides to show that beer mattered and that good beer was a drink that could soar to great heights. As Oliver said at the tasting, 'Beer has a wider range of flavours than wine. It is an incontrovertible, verified fact.'

In 1994 Oliver joined Brooklyn Brewery and embarked on an adventurous journey creating stylish innovative beers and pairing them with food. 'Every restaurant should have a beer menu', says Oliver. The brewery had been founded in 1987 by journalist Steve Hindy and banker Tom Potter and had played a huge part in breathing beer life back into New York's best-known borough. In 1898 there had been 40 breweries, and even in the 1960s one in ten of the beers drunk in the USA was brewed there. Times changed and by 1970 no breweries were left. And then, more than a decade later, along came Brooklyn Brewery.

Oliver chose the Sorachi hop, which had been developed by Dr Yoshitada Mori of the Sapporo brewery in Japan. Originally, it was a cross between two famed varieties, Brewers Gold and Saaz. It has never been grown in large quantities, either in Japan or in Washington State in the USA, but its qualities have captured the attention of many craft brewers. Oliver chose the hop because of its aromas of lemon zest and lemongrass. At his tasting at the White Horse pub, Oliver paired his Belgian saison-style beer with a goat's cheese. The lemon character of the beer melded perfectly with the tart silkiness of the cheese. It was a near perfect match.

Brooklyn Sorachi Ace is an unfiltered golden Belgian-style farmhouse ale with a wonderfully clean malt flavour. The beer is dry hopped, with the Sorachi added late in the production process. This releases an entrancing lemony-herbal scent. The malt is German pilsner and the beer is first fermented with a Belgian yeast before undergoing a secondary fermentation with a champagne yeast.

It's a summer's day in the glass and near perfect. Chefs who want to develop a beer and food menu should shun the world of industrial-style beers and take a sip of Sorachi Ace and marvel at its potential.

6. PLINY THE ELDER
Style: Double IPA
Strength: 8% ABV
Brewer: Russian River
Country of origin: USA
First brewed: 1999

When it comes to people using social media, this beer is a shining star. More than once, the beer has been voted the best in the world by internet voters. The American Homebrewers Association magazine, *Zymurgy*, named it America's Best Beer. And if that isn't enough, it was named top beer by the American Homebrewers Association for seven years in a row. The beer has class.

The beer's creator, Vinnie Cilurzo, describes it not just as an India Pale Ale, but an imperial, double one. Well it is bigger and bolder than most IPAs, and it has been stored for nine months in oak barrels that once contained wine. The wood adds a pronounced but entrancing sour note to the beer. *Brettanomyces* is a wonderful thing.

The beer is produced annually by the Russian River brewery, which was established in 1997, deep in the heart of California wine country. It is a bitter beer, measuring more than 100 International Bitterness Units (IBU), the scale used for measuring such things. Many lager-style beers nudge the bottom of the scale with an IBU of 10, and English bitter nudges higher with 24, while many so-called assertive IPAs top 50 IBUs.

This beer is a tribute to hops and their power for influencing the flavour of beers. Its name comes from the

© Russian River

Roman scholar who is reputed to have given the botanical name to hops. Pliny wrote the *Naturalis Historia*, which comprises 37 volumes and is one of the largest single works to have survived from the Roman Empire. Published more than 2,000 years ago, the collection was purported to have included every fact ever known.

A double IPA is one of the most popular beer styles brewed by the new wave of US craft brewers. Its roots go back to the English IPAs that were exported around the British Empire. But these beers are bigger in terms of strength and hoppiness than their English inspirations. An American would describe this beer as bigger and better than its across-the-pond predecessors. Pliny is constructed with Amarillo, Centennial, CTZ and Simcoe hops. But the assertive, aromatic hop bitterness is balanced by a full malt character.

Drinkers in California regard a double IPA as the ultimate beer style, with Pliny at the top of the plinth. Cilurzo first brewed a beer of this style when he was at the Blind Pig brewpub in Temecula, California. When he joined Russian River, he developed a new recipe and has continued to brew it annually.

According to Russian River, the beer was brewed for the world's first ever Double IPA festival in 2000 at the Bistro in Hayward, California. Ten brewers were invited, and six including Russian River had to brew something new. Cilurzo created a new version of the beer he had been brewing since 1994 in his previous job.

Russian River also brews a bigger version of the beer, known as the Younger. Stronger, it is 10 per cent ABV and it has even more hops in it. And to make it even more interesting and hard to get, it is only sold in the company's brewpub. Bigger than a double IPA, it is described as a triple. The beer uses different hops each year, but typically includes Simcoe,

Warrior, Chinook, Centennial, Amarillo and Tomahawk. It was first brewed as a winter seasonal back in the early 2000s, and like its elder brother it is now so successful the brewery is under pressure to brew both not just annually but all year around.

5. ARROGANT BASTARD ALE
Style: American strong ale
Strength: 7.2% ABV
Brewer: Stone
Country of origin: USA
First brewed: 1997

If the music is too loud, then you are too old.

Uncompromising is a good word to describe this beer. 'Hated by many, loved by a few' is a phrase the company uses to describe people's reaction to it.

The founders of Stone, Greg Koch and Steve Wagner, say they have been challenging convention since they first opened in 1996. In the beginning, unlike their beers, the company was not very big, but since they started as a small microbrewery, they have grown until they are now one of the largest craft brewers in the USA. And they have ambitious plans: a new brewery is being developed in Richmond, Virginia, and they have set their eyes on European expansion too. A new site has been opened in Berlin. The company is known for its bold, flavourful and largely hop-centric beers. And beer magazine *BeerAdvocate* named it the 'All-time Top Brewery on Planet Earth' twice in a poll of readers.

© Stone

The company began as a collaboration between home brewer Wagner and beer geek and wannabe rock 'n' roll entrepreneur Koch. The pair met first in Los Angeles in 1989, when they both worked in the music business. But it was some years later that they by chance met again at a weekend class on the sensory evaluation of beer at the University of California.

They kept in touch and over the years their conversations were always about beer and a shared dislike of fizzy lager. At the time, other like-minded beer warriors were setting up their own breweries. Koch and Wagner wanted to join in on the revolution. With the help of some family money and a lot of hard work, the pair set up their first brewpub San Marcos in 1996.

Wagner had spent a lot of time developing the recipes for the company's first beer, a pale ale. On sampling one of the early batches, he exclaimed to Koch, 'Oh god, I've really screwed up'. Possibly because he's a contrarian, Koch took the opposite view and declared, 'it's the best beer I've ever tasted'. Their conversation became more animated as they discussed the beer – joking that it was too good for most people. And so the seed corn for the marketing of the beer was born, including phrases like 'You're not worthy.' The Arrogant brand was developing.

They developed the idea of a beer that didn't appeal to the mainstream. Attitude was everything. And lines on the label such as 'This is an aggressive beer. You probably won't like it' won people over and created huge loyalty among the beer's fans.

The style of not caring what people thought of them as a way of winning and keeping loyalty is similar to the approach BrewDog took in Britain a generation later. The strategy created a deep loyalty among the drinkers who did like it.

Hops aren't just to the fore in a glass of Arrogant Bastard IPA, they assail the senses; but even though the International Bitterness Units top more than 100, the beer is surprisingly drinkable. The hop hit is kept in balance by a good, if simple, malt base that securely underpins the beer. The fruit and caramel sweetness are in harmony.

If you think you have 'taste and sophistication', then you should try this beer. But be prepared to give it time: the Arrogant Bastard will grow on you.

4. MILK STOUT
Style: Milk stout
Strength: 5.3% ABV
Brewer: Left Hand
Country of origin: USA
First brewed: 2001

There's only one way, and it's the Left Hand way.

Originally the company traded as Indian Peaks Brewing, but another company was using the name, so they had to change it. So the company took its new name from the Native American Arapaho Chief Niwot, which translates as Left Hand. The Chief played a major role in Colorado's history. He urged his tribe to live in peace with the white settlers. It was a policy that worked for many years until 1864, when a troop of US cavalry massacred the tribe.

Like many of the new wave of US brewers, the Left Hand story began with brewing at home. In 1990, co-founder Dick Doore was given a home brewing kit. His hobby became

an obsession, which took him to Colorado in August 1993, where he met up with an old friend, the other co-founder of the company, Eric Wallace. They began to collaborate on home brews, which were avidly consumed by neighbours. And then one night they had 'the' conversation: why don't we set up a commercial brewery?

The company was formally created in 1994 and they surprised even themselves by winning medals at the Great American Beer Festival that year – a gold for its Sawtooth Ale and a bronze for Black Jack Porter. Left Hand was on its way.

They shared a like for English-style beers, especially stout. And so the quest to brew the best milk stout in the world began. Their inspiration was Mackeson. It is a milk stout with a full, sweet taste with only a hint of malt. It was an incredibly successful beer in Britain at the start of the 20th century. The style was so called because it contains lactose or milk sugar. Lactose is not fermented by brewing yeasts, so it doesn't make alcohol but it does give a beer a full mouthfeel, without adding too much sugar-cloying flavour. These days the lactose is not derived from dairy products.

The beer is a harmonious partnership of chocolate and sweet roasted malt flavours. It's easy drinking and gently caresses the tongue. The finish is reassuring and dry with a coffee, cream flourish.

The company took milk stout to a new level in 2011 when it introduced Milk Stout Nitro in a bottle. The beer went down a storm at that year's Great American Beer Festival. They were the first craft brewers to master the art and skill of packaging beer with nitrogen. It is a technique that Guinness has used for many years. Using nitrogen makes a beer less carbonated and therefore less acidic, and it also helps create a fine head and a gorgeous mouthfeel.

3. GONZO IMPERIAL PORTER
Style: Imperial stout
Strength: 9.2% ABV
Brewer: Flying Dog
Country of origin: USA
First brewed: 2005

Wow. This is a big beer.

The beer was brewed as a tribute to the late writer Hunter S. Thompson, the man who created the gonzo style of journalism. Thompson, to put it mildly, was a man who lived life on the edge. A crime as a teenager saw him choose the US Air Force instead of a prison sentence. But life in uniform didn't suit him and he was discharged, so he decided to turn to journalism.

Thompson would have been a nightmare on a traditional news desk, where the journalist would have been a reporter on events and not part of the story. Instead, he went on to develop a style of writing that blurs fact and fiction and sees the writer at the heart of the story. His best-known work, *Fear and Loathing in Las Vegas*, epitomises the self-indulgent gonzo style as he frantically tells of a debauched drug-crazed weekend chasing the American dream in the early 1970s.

Flying Dog brewpub was founded in 1990 in Aspen, Colorado. Flying Dog's tribute to Thompson, Gonzo Imperial Porter, is much more than a token. The writer was a friend and drinking companion of the brewery's founder, George Stranahan. They met when Thompson was Stranahan's tenant, renting Owl Farm in Woody Creek, a small town outside of Aspen, Colorado, that would become Thompson's

© Flying Dog

'fortified compound'. Thompson and Stranahan talked politics, watched football, got drunk, shot guns and blew shit up. Although the beer is now brewed in Maryland, a long way from its original home, its creation in 2005 is seen as a fitting tribute to the writer.

Thompson's oft-time collaborator in his journalism was the English illustrator Ralph Steadman, who has designed the label, as he does for other Flying Dog beers. Steadman had drawn his first label for Flying Dog in 1995. Steadman's approach to art is as provocative as Thompson's was to writing. Flying Dog's approach to marketing and controversy then was similar to BrewDog's today. Steadman's first label was for Road Dog Porter, which included the strapline 'Good Beer, No Shit'. The phrase didn't go down well with the Colorado Liquor Board, who banned it.

The brewer's response was to change the line to 'Good Beer, No Censorship' and to enlist the help of the American Civil Liberties Union, who mounted a campaign for the original words to be used – a battle that was won in 2001. So after Thompson's suicide in 2005, it was only right that Steadman would create the image for the beer. The label portrays a skeletal image of someone holding a syringe.

Flying Dog's Imperial Porter is as big as Thompson's character, but nowhere as chaotic. It's a beer full of big flavours. Jet black to the eye with a golden brown-white head, the beer is full of dark fruit, chocolate and liquorice flavours from the cocktail of malts. Then come the hops, first Warrior and Northern Brewer bring a sweeping bitterness on a grand scale, then comes a blast of citrus notes from the Cascade.

At a recent British Guild of Beer Writers awards dinner, the beer was paired with a chocolate tower of walnuts, tonka beans and caramel. According to the menu notes, the coffee and chocolate notes and bitterness of the beer 'lifted the whole combination into a heavenly dimension'. And if the Imperial Porter is not enough, the brewery has also produced a barrel-aged version. The beer is put into oak whiskey barrels for a minimum of 180 days. It soars with vanilla and whiskey notes.

These are not beers to fear or loathe, they should be loved and revered. As it says on the label, 'OK! Let's party!!'

2. PALE ALE
Style: American pale ale
Strength: 5.6% ABV
Brewer: Sierra Nevada
Country of origin: USA
First brewed: 1980

Is this the most important beer brewed in the last 40 years? Arguably, the influence of this beer is as profound as the introduction of the first golden pils in Pilsen by Josef Groll in 1842. Today, Sierra Nevada's classic has often been mimicked, but rarely bettered.

Many people remember the first time they tasted this beer. Its fragrant, floral aromas are so distinct, it stands out from a crowd. In my case, I was blind-tasting it for a major supermarket in the UK. I immediately wanted to find out who had brewed it and how.

It is a beer that succinctly encapsulates the spirit of adventure and desire to be different that captured the new wave of brewers of the late 1970s. The world was getting the taste for hop forward and boldly flavoured beers.

The beer's creator, Ken Grossman, started to brew at home. His original desire was simply to brew beers he wanted to drink. He learnt the rudiments of brewing from the father of a close friend. A lifetime's journey had begun. He was hooked by the sweet smell of malt being mashed and the release of fragrant aromas when hops were added to the boil. And then there was the magic of fermentation, which turned the sweet liquid into beer.

The 1970s were a golden age for California – even though the state was subject to severe drought, which limited water supplies. A new generation started to develop their own counterculture; for many this meant skateboarding, for Grossman it was cycling and brewing.

Originally from Southern California, Grossman in 1972 was on a cycling trip along the north coast of California. He decided to visit some friends who were students at California State University in Chico. He fell in love with the ethos, aspirations and dreams of the people of the town and decided this was where he wanted to live.

Successful social countercultures invoke social change. And Grossman's agent of change was going to be beer. As he says on his company's website: 'We started small, with a homebrew shop, a love of American hops and plenty of passion. In the process, we changed the beer world forever. Decades later, we're still at it, and the passion burns brighter than ever.'

In 1976, capturing the mood of the time, as exemplified by the publication of the handbook of the counterculture, the *Whole Earth Catalog*, Grossman opened a home brew supply shop in Chico. He was starting a journey that was to alter the interests and lifestyles of millions of people. The Home Brew Shop was run with a fellow brewer, Paul Camusi, and was an ideal place for Grossman to practise his craft: people would come and visit to try the beer.

Sourcing the ingredients for beer was always difficult, especially hops, in the relatively small quantities he needed. But rather than wait for them to come to him, he drove to the mountain. Hops were grown north of Chico in the Washington State region of Yakima. He smooth-talked some hop brokers into selling him 40 kg of 'brewers cuts' – samples sent to breweries to try before purchasing bales. He returned with the whole floral cone hops for which Sierra Nevada is now renowned. The Cascade hop is now known worldwide for its intense citrus and pine flavours and it was to become the signature accent in his beers. Today, it defines the west coast style of brewing.

By the end of the 1970s, he had fashioned the plans for a commercial brewery. Brewing beer commercially had to be on a much larger scale than home brewing for a few friends. Tanks were sourced from dairies and many brews were tried and discarded. The beer that is now widely available today was finely honed. It's strong but not too extreme. It pours a dark amber in the glass and has a recognisable fragrant bouquet and spicy flavour.

Today the Chico site produces more than 1.2 million hectolitres of beer a year and Sierra Nevada has a second site near Asheville, North Carolina. Big it might have become, but it doesn't seem to have strayed from its countercultural roots. It is committed to quality, integrity, use of the very best ingredients, doing things properly and, above all, caring for its environment.

The company has a greener than green 'no waste' policy, has one of America's largest arrays of solar panels, and is using some of its profits to support the Trappist monastery New Clairvaux in the small Californian town of Vina.

Passion, innovation and a willingness to push at boundaries are attributes that have served the company well.

1. TWELVE DAYS

Style: Ale
Strength: 5.5% ABV
Brewer: Hook Norton
Country of origin: UK
First brewed: 1992

Is this really the best beer in the world? Well, I've sampled hundreds if not thousands of beers over the years. But in the last twelve months more than 15,000 beers have been brewed in the UK alone, and as hard as I have tried, I haven't sampled them all. And now with more than 30,000 brewers in the world, it's an almost impossible task to try one beer from each. To achieve that would mean having more than 80 beers a day for a whole year. It would be a difficult and probably dangerous task.

However, there are several reasons for making this 'my' best beer. Twelve Days is a beer from one of the local brewers in my home county of Oxfordshire. It is a beer that has history, provenance and integrity. It is created at the unique Hook Norton brewery in the village of the same name in north Oxfordshire. Here, progress is measured by pints and the gentle clip clop of horses' hooves, as the brewery's horse-drawn dray delivers beer to some of its local pubs.

Hook Norton is a brewery forged in the past, which lives in the present and is looking to the future. It is a brewery that still has one family beating at its heart. The Clarke family established it in 1856 and now six generations on they are still intimately involved with the brewing of the beer.

It is a brewery steeped in memories. The current brewery

may seem old and traditional, but in 1876 when it was designed by the great brewery architect William Bradford, it would have been seen as an engineering wonder of its time, as modern and exciting as an iPhone 6.

It was originally powered by a steam engine, installed in 1899, which is still occasionally fired up today: an act that seems to shake the building to its 19th-century foundations. The raw materials were hauled up to the top of a tower. Water was at the summit, underneath were the bags of malted barley and the grist mill. Slowly as each part of the process of making a beer – mashing, fermentation, maturation and racking – took place, gravity would stage by stage draw everything down and around the building.

This tactile, elemental process is still followed today. In its heyday much of the equipment would have been made of iron, copper and wood, rather than stainless steel and plastic. But as the present-day managing director, James Clarke, says, his great great grandfather would have used stainless steel, and no doubt quality plastic too, if it had been available.

Like all the other beers in this book, Twelve Days is made by brewers who care about the ingredients they've chosen and they treat them with reverence. Good beer and its ingredients should be respected.

Twelve Days was created by a young James Clarke in 1992, a year after he had joined the family-owned brewery. One of the first jobs he was given was to create a new seasonal ale for sale during winter months. He decided to create a strong bitter, which was finely balanced and mouth-warming. At first the dark brown strong beer didn't have a name. Instead, until the name Twelve Days was hit on, each cask simply had a handwritten label stuck to it saying 'Christmas Ale'.

For the mash, Clarke chose Maris Otter pale ale, chocolate, crystal and enzymic malts. Four chords that create a complex

song of fruit and nuts, cinnamon and spice. It is a bronzed god of a beer, full of nut and fruit flavours. A chorus of orange and spice is present in the aftertaste, which is dominated by a refreshing Golding and Challenger hops' bitter sweetness. It's liquid Christmas pudding in a glass.

Often when I am travelling and in a faraway airport or city, or on an aeroplane, where there is little choice of beer, I yearn for a drink like Twelve Days. I want something to remind me of my home, my family and my country's great pubs.

Twelve Days becomes a siren calling me home. It is a beautiful but dangerously drinkable strong beer. It is music and song in a glass, which whispers seductively in my ear, 'Try me, sip me, caress me with your tongue. I am waiting for you at home.' But my siren, unlike the mythical muses of Greece, will not entrap my body and soul in a fatal lethargy, it will set me free. And it appeals to my spirit and my flesh.

It is a beer that is irresistible, one with an enchanting call. Its lure could calm the winds and fly me home. I yearn for the moment when I can lift a glass of Twelve Days to my lips. It means I've arrived home and I've missed it. It's my local beer. I want its strong, fruit-sweet tones to flow over my lips. Few who listen to this beer's call can resist it.

Everyone should have a local beer. And it should be a great beer. One that reminds them of their memories, hopes and aspirations. Every brewer should be on a mission to make their beer the best in the world. Great beers spark conversations, encourage laughter and underpin our memories.

Great beers, search for them as you would for silver, seek them out like hidden treasures. Seek them and find them. Beers, they're coming home; they're what life is all about. Locally brewed, but loved worldwide.